Richard J. Hutchings

Brodie's Notes on

Tennyson:
Selected Poetry

Pan Books London and Sydney

First published 1979 by Pan Books Ltd
Cavaye Place, London SW10 9PG
1 2 3 4 5 6 7 8 9
© Richard J. Hutchings 1979
ISBN 0 330 50157 7
Filmset in Great Britain by
Northumberland Press Ltd, Gateshead, Tyne and Wear
Printed by
Richard Clay (The Chaucer Press) Ltd, Bungay, Suffolk

Contents

Page references in these Notes are to the
Macdonald and Evans paperback edition of Tennyson:
Poems of 1842, the Oxford University Press paperback edition of
Tennyson: Selected Poems and the Faber paperback edition of
A Choice of Tennyson's Verse.

To the student

A close reading of the poems is the student's primary task. These Notes will help to increase your understanding and appreciation of the poems, and to stimulate *your own* thinking about them. *The Notes are in no way intended as a substitute* for a thorough knowledge of the poetry.

Introduction

There is no better way of introducing *Notes* on Tennyson, or in fact on any poet, than by quoting what he himself once remarked: 'Poetry is like shot-silk with many glancing colours. Every reader must find his own interpretation according to his ability, and according to his sympathy with the poet.' It is well to remember that the more familiar the student becomes with a poem, the clearer becomes his understanding of what the poet intended to express or convey to him. It is only by reading and re-reading with a totally receptive mind, exercising at the same time the critical faculties, that poetry may be enjoyed – which is its purpose.

The poem summaries and textual notes have been divided into two parts. Part 1 consists of the *Poems of 1842*, arranged in alphabetical order of titles. The poems in Part 2 are arranged in chronological order, the latter representing the last two phases in the poet's development (see the section on 'The Poet and his Work').

The poet and his work

The Reverend George Clayton Tennyson, incumbent of the adjoining parishes of Somersby and Bag Enderby in the wolds of north Lincolnshire, had eleven children, seven boys and four girls. The three eldest were Frederick, Charles and Alfred, all to become poets of considerable talent. Outstanding among them was Alfred, born on 6 August 1809.

Although educated away from home for five years at Louth Grammar School, a strictly 'if you spare the rod you'll spoil the child' establishment, the Tennyson boys' sound classical schooling and fanatical interest in poetry was the direct result of their father's tuition at home in Somersby Rectory. But George Tennyson was a morose, moody and sometimes violent man, particularly after excessive drinking. His father had forced him to take Holy Orders, and all his life virtually ignored him in favour of his younger brother, who was to become an affluent Member of Parliament.

As the Tennyson family increased, the house became so crowded that by 1818, in order to accommodate the twenty-five occupants (including servants) the family were compelled to sleep five or six to a room. It is hardly surprising that George Tennyson, with his natural melancholia, should have taken to drink. However, notwithstanding the deep flaws in his makeup, he educated eleven brilliant children before he died in 1831, and was largely responsible for stimulating the genius of one of our greatest poets.

In 1827 Charles and Alfred, with Frederick's assistance, produced a volume of poetry entitled *Poems by Two Brothers*: Jacksons of Louth were the courageous publishers. All three boys went up to Cambridge, where, at Trinity, Alfred was awarded the Chancellor's Medal for the poem 'Timbuctoo'.

While there he was admitted to the company of the Apostles, an élite group of intellectuals who debated and discussed politics, religion and literature. He became the intimate friend of Arthur Henry Hallam, the brilliant son of the historian Henry Hallam; together, in 1830, they toured the Pyrenees and gave financial aid to the Spanish revolutionaries who were attempting to overthrow the king. In the same year Alfred published *Poems, chiefly Lyrical*, which was severely criticized by 'Christopher North' in *Blackwood's Magazine*.

Hallam was engaged to Alfred's sister Emily, but during a tour in Austria in 1833 he was taken ill suddenly, and died. Alfred was distraught at the news, and began to write a series of elegies in memory of his friend. At the same time he wrote 'Two Voices', 'Ulysses', 'St Simeon Stylites', 'St Agnes' Eve', 'Lancelot and Queen Guinevere', 'Sir Galahad' and 'The Beggar Maid'. He had also begun work on *Morte d'Arthur*. His *Poems* (1833) provoked a vitriolic attack by John Wilson Crocker in the *Quarterly Review*.

Alfred was particularly sensitive to criticism of his work at this stage, so much so that he published nothing until 1842, when he brought out, in two volumes, the important *Poems of 1842*. The collection had no immediate impact on the critics, but gradually discerning lovers of poetry recognized a new poetic genius.

Nevertheless, Alfred's problems were numerous. After his father's death he automatically assumed responsibility for the Tennyson family – by that time almost penniless. They left Somersby in 1837, staying first at High Beech, Epping, where he became re-acquainted with old university friends. In 1840 he unwisely invested some inherited money in a machine wood-carving project initiated by a certain Doctor Allen. This collapsed, but fortunately for the poet a newfound friend, Lushington, had insured against just such a loss. Lushington was to marry Tennyson's sister Cecilia, in 1842.

The poet had by now become so depressed that the family moved to Cheltenham to be near a hydropathic hospital, where he received treatment. Realizing their desperate straits, Henry Hallam, his late friend's father, appealed to Sir Robert Peel to allow Alfred a £200 Civil List pension, to which Sir Robert willingly agreed. With this encouragement Tennyson gradually recovered his health and was soon engaged in researching the Arthurian legends in the West Country. He felt, however, that he was perhaps not yet mature enough in his art to begin work on such a gigantic epic. Instead, he applied his mind to the theme of women's equality, not only in society but in education. *The Princess*, containing some of the most delightful lyrics he ever wrote, was completed in 1847.

Within the next three years he renewed his friendship with Emily Sellwood, to whom he had formerly been engaged. The engagement had been broken off because of Tennyson's lack of prospects; but it was soon renewed when Emily had a chance to read Alfred's 'Elegies', as he called them. By 1849 the 'Elegies' were completed and Emily suggested that the poem should be renamed *In Memoriam A.H.H.* It was published in 1850 and ran into three editions that same year.

Emily and Alfred Tennyson were married at Shiplake on 13 June 1850, and together they went on a pilgrimage to the little church in Clevedon where Arthur Henry Hallam was buried in 1834. The poet had addressed these lines to Emily in *In Memoriam* (stanza 95):

You say, but with no touch of scorn,
Sweet-hearted, you, whose light-blue eyes
Are tender over drowning flies,
You tell me, doubt is Devil-born.
I know not: one indeed I knew
In many a subtle question versed,
Who touched a jarring lyre at first,
But ever strove to make it true:

Perplext in faith, but pure in deeds,
At last he beat his music out.
There lives more faith in honest doubt,
Believe me, than in half the creeds.

The turning-point in Tennyson's career had come at the age of forty-one. His marriage was happy, and *In Memoriam* a great success. On the death of Wordsworth, Tennyson succeeded him as Poet Laureate. He proved to be the Poet Laureate *par excellence*. However, after he was appointed in 1850 he seldom allowed himself to forget that, primarily, he was a God-gifted poet, and that the laureateship must always be of secondary importance in his life; that poetry must always supersede praise in his official duties. Despite this he was genuinely fond of Queen Victoria and her Consort, and in the year following his appointment dedicated a new edition of *In Memoriam* to her.

This is not to say that Tennyson emulated Wordsworth and avoided laureate pieces entirely, but his work always bore the stamp of his individual genius and was generally conceived from genuine inspiration. He loved England and her people, and could evoke in his poetry the glorious pageantry of her history, as seen in *Idylls of the King* (1859). But Tennyson did not live in the past; he was very involved in the contemporary scene – with the death of the Duke of Wellington, the French threats of invasion, the advancement of science and the expansion and development of Britain's colonies. A number of what would seem to have been laureate pieces were, in fact, not written to order at all – in particular, the 'Ode on the Death of the Duke of Wellington' (1852) and 'The Charge of the Light Brigade' (1854).

Friendship and mutual respect existed between Prince Albert and the Poet Laureate on a man-to-man rather than a royal master-to-servant footing. The Consort found his ideal in the King Arthur of *Idylls of the King*, whose example he attempted to follow. Tennyson believed that he succeeded very well in doing so, a point he stresses in the Dedication of the 1862 edition.

In Memoriam apart, *Idylls of the King* did more to strengthen the ties of genuine friendship between the royal family and the Laureate than any other of his poems. In one of Prince Albert's last letters from Buckingham Palace, written on the 17 May 1860, which was accompanied by a copy of the *Idylls*, he asked the poet to autograph it, and added:

'They quite kindle the feeling with which the legends of King Arthur must have inspired the chivalry of old, whilst the graceful form in which they are presented blends those feelings with the softer tone of our own age ...

Three years after his appointment as Poet Laureate, Tennyson settled happily at Farringford, Freshwater, in the Isle of Wight, with his wife and first son, Hallam. Lionel was born in 1854. The eternal round of socializing in London with literary friends had begun to interfere with the progress of his work, and the obstacle of the Solent was sufficient, he believed, to deter the less welcome City acquaintances from calling on him. The island environment provided the ideal stimulus and topographical detail for his monodrama, *Maud* (1855) and the popular *Enoch Arden* (1864). It was there that he began his magnum opus, *Idylls of the King*.

Tennyson had now reached maturity, and gained a new confidence in his work; he was acknowledged nationally as the poet of the people. On the Isle of Wight so many hero-worshipping tourists plagued his life that, in order to escape them, he was forced to build a summer residence in a secluded part of West Sussex. The move proved beneficial in that he completed 'The Holy Grail' (1869), an essential part of the *Idylls* that had eluded him for so long. This achievement marked the successful end of the second phase of his career.

Building began on Tennyson's new house, 'Aldworth', in

Sussex in September 1868. About this time he added more sections to his *Idylls*; 'The Coming of Arthur' was completed in 1869, then came 'Pelleas and Ettarre', the new 'Morte D'Arthur', 'Gareth and Lynette', 'The Last Tournament', 'Balin and Balan' and lines added to 'Merlin and Vivien'. All this occupied his time until 1885 but by 1875 Tennyson felt it was high time for experiment. He determined to produce poetic drama for the stage at the risk of losing popularity as a lyric and ballad writer. First came *Queen Mary* (1875), followed by *Harold* (1877) and *Becket* (1884), the latter eventually proving a tremendous success not only on the stage but also as a literary work. Following these were the poetic comedy *The Cup and the Falcon* (1884) and the prose drama *The Promise of May* (1886). In 1888 he suffered a bad attack of rheumatic gout but continued to work. *The Foresters* was successfully launched in New York in 1892, the year of his death at Aldworth.

Not all of this period was devoted to dramatic works; Tennyson also produced some fine ballads and lyrics and of these perhaps the best remembered is 'Crossing the Bar' (1889).

Further reading

The Tennysons: Background to Genius, Charles Tennyson and Hope Dyson (Macmillan)

Language and Structure in Tennyson's Poetry, J. B. Priestley (Deutsch)

Poems of Tennyson, edited by Christopher Ricks (Longman)

Studies in Tennyson, Henry van Dyke (Kennikat, New York)

Influences on style and structure

When Tennyson was born at Somerby rectory, the Romantic revival of English poetry – largely initiated by the *Lyrical Ballads* of Wordsworth and Coleridge – was only twelve years old. Byron, Shelley and Keats grew to maturity in their art during Tennyson's childhood and youth, and had a profound influence on him. It is not surprising, then, that he was captivated by Byron's virile style and romantic individualism, as he was by Shelley's splendour and colour. But he was soon to reject their influence.

Of the five Romantic poets, he found most to admire and emulate in the eldest and youngest of their number: Wordsworth for his breadth of vision, mystical communion with Nature, but essential simplicity; and Keats for his sublime dedication to Beauty and Truth. In his wisdom, he used a little of each as the foundation for his own poetic talents. Tennyson benefited from his deep romantic susceptibility to Nature. There is something of the painter in his graphic use of words to produce the impression of a scene's true outline and colour. His realism and precision of detail are reflections of his times. New scientific knowledge and discoveries, and the rapid expansion and development of Britain's colonies, were awakening influences that were reflected in the poet's work. Like Wordsworth, he experienced the mysterious relationship between man and his environment, where 'the outer in-animate world is felt to be the resemblance and reflection of human moods'.

By 1809 the republican ideals generated in Wordsworth by the French Revolution of 1789 had soured into disillusion-ment. French hopes for liberty, equality and the brotherhood of all men (which had appealed to many just Englishmen) were seen at the beginning of the nineteenth century to be no more than the springs of a new tyranny far bloodier than anything Europe had ever known. Cheated now of the fulfilment of their democratic dreams, Englishmen no longer cared much for the fate of their society – already in 1802 Wordsworth had cried in anguish to the spirit of a Milton to save England from her torpor, from the spiritual, intellectual and moral bankruptcy evident everywhere: 'Milton! thou shouldst be living at this hour . . .'

A few years later Byron and Shelley began waging private wars against the social system of their day. The voices of poets were largely unheard, and the Anglican Church offered no inspiring leadership. Tennyson understood well that England's greatest spiritual need was the reaffirmation of basic Christian beliefs, and that only in this way could she rid herself of the cursed 'albatross' of her troubled conscience. The poet with his religious faith – so often put to test in his youth – sensed that he would be able to help with this. But his first volume, *Poems of Two Brothers*, was strongly influenced by Byron's work, and revealed that he was not yet ready for the task.

The long-awaited social reform came in the 1830s, from which developed the High and Broad Church movements of the Anglican faith. It was during the era of this spiritual rebirth that the poetical careers of Tennyson and Browning had their faltering beginnings. Two churchmen, J. H. Newman and Frederick Maurice, educated at Oxford and Cambridge respectively, befriended and influenced Tennyson, and helped to sustain and broaden his faith. Perhaps Maurice had the greater influence, revealing to him the necessary vitality of the present, the deep need for high poetic work – man alive and Nature alive with the life of God – which were part of Maurice's doctrine. Tennyson learned also the importance of 'self-reverence, self-knowledge, self-control'. Another great influence on the poet was the Christian socialism of Charles Kingsley.

The death of his friend Hallam in September 1833 was to shake violently the foundations of Tennyson's faith, to scar his memory with sadness at the loss of a man of potential genius, who would not only have risen to greatness but on whom he had leaned for courage and support under the vitriolic attacks of bigoted literary critics. His professional literary career began in earnest with the publication of *In Memoriam*, elegies resulting from his grief at the loss of Hallam, in which he described 'the way of the soul'.

Like Wordsworth with Coleridge, Arthur Hallam and Tennyson had planned to collaborate in writing a volume of poetry, something in the style of the *Lyrical Ballads*, but Hallam's father talked them out of the idea. Instead, Tennyson brought out *Poems, chiefly Lyrical* (1830), which contained an early version of some of his finest verse (which he later revised).

Hallam, though an intimate friend of Tennyson, could review the book dispassionately but with enthusiasm in *The Englishman's Magazine* (August 1831):

'Mr Tennyson belongs decidedly to the class we have already described as Poets of Sensation. He sees all the forms of Nature with the *eruditus oculus*, and his ear has a fairy fineness. There is a strange earnestness in his worship of beauty, which throws a charm over his impassioned song, more easily felt than described, and not to be escaped by those who have once felt it . . . . . We have remarked five distinctive excellencies of his own manner. First, his luxuriance of imagination, and at the same time his control over it. Secondly, his power of embodying himself in ideal characters, or rather moods of character, with such extreme accuracy and adjustment that the circumstances of narrative seem to have a natural correspondence with the predominant feeling, and, as it were, to be evolved from it by assimilative force. Thirdly, his vivid, picturesque delineation of objects, and the peculiar skill with which he holds all of them fused, to borrow a metaphor from science, in a medium of strong emotion. Fourthly, the variety of his lyrical measures, and exquisite modulation of harmonious sounds and cadences to the swell and fall of the feelings expressed. Fifthly, the elevated habits of thought implied in these compositions, and imparting a mellow soberness of tone, more impressive to our minds than if the author had drawn up a set of opinions in verse, and sought to instruct the understanding rather than to communicate the love of beauty to the heart.'

Hallam had frequently visited Somersby in winter and summer, and in the year of his graduation at Cambridge he became engaged to Emily Tennyson, the poet's sister. Hallam had then lived at Wimpole Street, and after leaving Cambridge he studied law. In August 1833 he accompanied his father to Germany and then to Austria; the weather had been appalling, and Hallam contracted an intermittent fever that resulted in his sudden death in Vienna on 15 September: 'In Vienna's fatal walls/God's finger touch'd him, and he slept.'

Tennyson spoke later of the manner in which *In Memoriam* was written: that it was 'so queer that if there were a blank space I would put in a poem'. This, in fact, is what *In Memoriam* is: a jigsaw puzzle of the soul that took him seventeen years to complete. Or, to pre-empt Charles Darwin, it was the Natural Selection of the soul or faith as it evolved from the primordial state of abject morbid grief into a genuine strong belief in the existence of an immortal, all-knowing, all-loving Being.

Judging from Tennyson's *Poems of 1842* one is immediately struck by the extent of his reading and his knowledge of the classics and Greek mythology, which found expression in 'The Lotos-Eaters' and 'Choric Song', in 'Ulysses', 'Amphion', 'Tithonus' and 'Oenone'. He also tackled the ode form with equal success in 'Ode to Memory', delightful vignettes of girls in 'Claribel', 'Lilian', 'Isabel', 'Mariana', 'Adeline' and others, mood-verses, ballads, nature poems; but what he truly excelled in were lyrics. The second volume of *Poems of 1842* contained some of his most memorable pieces: 'Morte d'Arthur', 'The Gardener's Daughter', 'Locksley Hall', the already mentioned 'Ulysses', 'Sir Galahad', 'Break, Break, Break' and 'Come not when I am Dead', to name but a few.

In the same year as the publication of these two volumes, his sister Cecilia married Edmund Lushington (see the epithalamium of *In Memoriam*). Tennyson had become reconciled to the death of Arthur Hallam; the wound of grief had almost healed and he was beginning to regard the future with greater optimism and, above all, his faith in a loving God and a knowledge of the soul's immortality had restored confidence in himself and his work.

In common with *In Memoriam*, works like *Idylls of the King*, *Maud* and *The Princess* were composed and revised piecemeal, and as a result *Idylls* and *In Memoriam* suffered from a lack of continuity between the separate sections. His first essays on the Arthurian theme, as in 'The Lady of Shalott', 'Galahad' and 'Morte d'Arthur' had been purely Romantic in treatment, but the later *Idylls*, published in 1859, were allegories representing King Arthur as 'the ideal in the Soul of Man coming in contact with the warring elements of the flesh'. These showed the different ways in which men regard Conscience, 'some reverencing it as a heaven-born king, others ascribing to it an earthly origin'. Hallam Tennyson explained that his father had made the old legends his own, and had infused into them a spirit of modern thought and of ethical significance, setting his characters in a rich and varied landscape – indeed, had it been otherwise these archaic stories would never have achieved their worldwide appeal.

However, this attempt in the *Idylls* to cast an ancient (and possibly mythical) king as a modern-day ethical preacher – however beautifully disguised – was an inescapable weakness in the eyes of some Victorian realists; the famous literary biographer Sir Alfred Lyall (1830–89) pointed out, 'Not everyone has been able to overcome the effect of incongruity produced by a poem which invests the legendary personages of mediaeval romance with morals and manners of a fastidious delicacy and promotes them to an embodiment of our own ethical ideals.'

It should be remembered that Tennyson's childhood and upbringing were thoroughly imbued with Christian doctrine and moral ethics. Although his early poems were a temporary escape into myth and romance, in later years his verse is packed with biblical references and analogies, indicating just how extensive had been his theological training. Not surprisingly, then, from 1850 onwards his work adopts a more moral tone, particularly noticeable when comparing the early and later styles of approach to the Arthurian legends, in the change from the romantic and lyrical to the later allegories. The poet had grown away from his romantic roots, the emotional traumas and domestic instability of the early years, to the settled mature state induced by marriage, financial security and public recognition as the foremost poet of the day. Having assimilated Romanticism, a new poet evolved.

The last phase, of writing poetic drama for the stage, was a mistake, but worth trying. Other great Victorian poets had also attempted it, without success. The poet's forte was the romantic lyric and ballad; in his later years, when his popularity began to wane, he realized this. His great friend Edward Fitzgerald had always preferred the pre-1842 work which, he said, had 'a champagne quality' about it; and he told Tennyson as much.

Aspects of style

We have seen how much Tennyson was influenced by the times in which he lived, and by religious and poetical trends. But how much was his poetical style the man himself? Because of the simplicity and lucidness of his style, there is perhaps less need, when studying Tennyson, for the biographical preparation required for poets whose work is more obscure and ambiguous. Nevertheless, it may be helpful to see the man through the eyes of one of his best friends.

The writer and historian Thomas Carlyle (1795–1881) once described Tennyson as 'one of the finest looking men in the world – a great shock of rough dusky dark hair; bright, laughing hazel eyes; massive aquiline face, most massive yet most delicate; of sallow brown complexion, almost Indian looking; clothes cynically loose, free-and-easy, smokes infinite tobacco. His voice is musical, metallic, fit for loud laughter and piercing wail, and all that may lie between; speech and speculation free and plenteous; I do not meet in these late decades such company over a pipe!'

Though we find in Tennyson's poetry reflections of the great works of Milton, Homer, Theocritus, Virgil, Horace, Lucretius, Catullus, Ovid, Sappho, Alcman, Pindar, Aeschylus, Moschus, Callimachus, Quintus Smyrnaeus and possibly Simonides and Sophocles (where the classics are concerned); and the Old and New Testaments in everything he wrote – not to mention the old and young Romantics – his essential quality was his simplicity and lucidity of style. The literary critic and writer, Dr Stopford Brooke (1832–1916) confirms this:

The way in which he wrote, his choice of subjects, his style, were all the revelation of a character drawn on large and uncomplicated lines; and in this sense, in the complete sincerity to his inner being of all he did and in the manner of its doing, he was simple in the truest sense of the word.' Nothing was ever done for effect; no subject in which he was not veritably involved was taken up . . . The thing shaped was the legitimate child of natural thought and natural feeling. Vital sincerity or living correspondence between idea and form, that absolute necessity for all fine art as for all noble life, was his, and it is contained in what I call his simplicity.

Although highly intelligent, Tennyson was not a profound philosopher. He wrote of the love and duty of man and woman, of the myriad shades of human inter-relationships, and he succeeded in revealing beauty of thought, tenderness of feeling and exquisiteness of form. One mark of the great writer is his economy with words and a fitness of phrase. Tennyson's morality and sincerity were unquestionable, his workmanship curiously level from youth to age. His brooding and melancholia were always apparent, especially in his pre-1850 poetry (e.g. 'Break, Break, Break', 'Tears, Idle Tears' and, of course, *In Memoriam*).

Tennyson's technique ranged through the whole gamut of poetic devices to convey pathos, the magic of romantic myth, communion with Nature, love and heartbreak, sensual passion, abject suicidal grief, *joie de vivre*, perplexing doubts in the Christian faith, yet belief in the divine will and love of God. These and other moods and thoughts require fine handling; no amount of poetic technique succeeds without inherent imagination and that rare inspirational genius that, unquestionably, Tennyson had in large measure.

After the early 1830s, Tennyson's poetic technique became almost faultless in achieving the *mood* of a poem. He achieved euphony with such onomatopoeic devices as alliteration, assonance, sibilance, internal and conventional rhyming, with the emphasis of particular words or phrases (e.g. the songs from *The Princess*) and by overlapping rhymes between stanzas.

His blank verse deserves special attention. The poet himself has some words to say on this, and on alliteration: (from Hallam Tennyson's *Memoir* of the poet, Volume II)

The English public think that blank verse is the easiest thing in the world to write, mere prose cut up into five-foot lines; whereas it is one of the most difficult. In blank verse you can have from three up to eight beats; but, if you vary the beats unusually, your ordinary newspaper critic sets up a howl. The varying of the beats, of the construction of the feet, of the emphasis, of the extra-metrical syllables and of the pauses, helps to make the greatness of blank verse. There are many other things besides, for instance a fine ear for vowel-sounds, and the kicking of the geese out of the boat (i.e. doing away with sibilations); but few educated men really understand the structure of blank verse. I never put two *s*s together in any verse of mine. My line is not, as often quoted, 'And freedom broaden*s s*lowly down' – but 'And freedom slowly broadens down'. People sometimes say how 'studiedly alliterative' Tennyson's verse is. Why when I spout my lines first they come out so alliteratively that I have sometimes no end of trouble to get rid of the alliteration.

Writing in April 1843 in the *Edinburgh*, James Spedding remarked: 'The decade during which Mr Tennyson has remained silent has wrought a great improvement. The handling in his later pieces is much lighter and freer; the interest deeper and purer; there is more humanity with less image and drapery; a closer adherence to truth; a greater reliance for effect upon the simplicity of Nature.'

Symbolism is used extensively throughout Tennyson's work, as illustrated in 'The Lady of Shalott' where, through the influence of love, images are exchanged for reality. The poet invokes periods of history by using specific metre (e.g. the Homeric and Spenserian metres for poems based on Greek mythology) or with archaic forms of the language (e.g. the use of 'mine', 'thine', 'thee' etc., and the suffix '-eth') for romantic Arthurian pieces.

For changes of mood or stance within a poem Tennyson

varied rhyme or scansion (e.g. in 'The Vision of Sin', or in *Maud* where it is very necessary). And a change of beat within a stanza was often adopted to avoid monotony in the repetition of names (e.g. 'The Ballad of Oriana'). He even resorted on many occasions to false rhyming – that is, using the impure eye-rhyming as with 'forth' and 'worth', and 'shut' and 'put' (e.g. in 'The Day-Dream') – a habit he acquired from both generations of Romantics. Everything considered, Tennyson's poetry, in its ornament and rhythm, derived much from the arts of painting and music.

Poem summaries, textual notes and revision questions

Part 1

(*Note to the student:* As the following poems are taken from the three different set books, we have placed to the right of each title, in brackets, 'F + a page number', or 'ME + a page number', or 'OUP + a page number' – according to whether the poem is taken from the Faber, the Macdonald & Evans or the Oxford University Press edition, sometimes from two and occasionally from all three.)

Adeline (ME 40)

A delightful vignette of a girl's character. Adeline is all mystery and purity. With her faint Mona Lisa smile, rose lips and full blue eyes, she tugs remorselessly at the poet's heart. What thoughts, he reflects, do those distant dreamy eyes conceal? Is she a mythical creature, perhaps a Naiad – 'a phantom two hours old/Of a maiden passed away . . .?

This imaginative piece should be read in conjunction with the poem 'Margaret'. Possibly the character of Adeline may have been taken from Byron's *Don Juan*, Canto 13, in which Adeline, the wife of Lord Henry Amundeville, was 'not indifferent, but hid her feelings under a cold presence'. See also Milton's *Paradise Lost*, Book 4, line 162 and Isaiah 45,14.

Naiad Water nymph.
Sabaean Arabian.
carcanet Necklace.
Letters cowslips on the hill The poet explains this by saying that the red spots on the cowslip bell appear to resemble a fairy alphabet.

Amphion (F 96; ME 238)

In Greek mythology, Amphion was one of the twin sons of
Zeus and Antiope. So magical was his lute-playing that he
was said to have built the city of Thebes by his music alone:
the stones danced, of their own accord, into the construction
of walls and houses. And trees came down the mountains –
while bushes and flowers ascended from the valleys – to
furnish the new city with plant life.

   The poet grieves that such marvels are no longer possible;
he resigns himself to months of toil and cultivation, for he is
no Amphion – and poets must also do physical work.

scion Branch.
limber Flexible, resilient.
briony-vine Vine of the briar.
linden Lime.
woodbine wreaths Honeysuckle.
gallopaded i.e. *gallopade*, a lively Middle-Eastern dance.
coterie Circle or set.
Poussetting Dancing round hand in hand.
scirrhous Cancerous or cankerous.
Van Diemen Tasmania was originally named Van Diemen's
   Land after Anton van Diemen, governor of the Dutch East
   Indies, 1636 to 1645.

Audley Court (ME 168)

This dramatic idyll was written in Torquay in 1838, and
should be studied in conjunction with 'Walking to the Mail'
and 'Will Waterproof's Lyrical Monologue'. The simplicity
of language and dramatic content suggest strongly the influence of Wordsworth and the ideals of the Romantic
revival.

   It is the story of a day's outing and picnic at Audley
Court grounds in which the poet is accompanied by Francis

Hale, a farmer who lives across the bay. Failing to find rooms for the night at the *Bull* or the *Fleece*, the two men decide to return to Audley Court, which was familiar to them from the past. They discuss how life has treated them and their friends. They note the lack of game at Audley Court, whereas it had once been plentiful. Systems of agriculture and politics also occupy them, on which they argue hotly. But soon they are on amicable, laughing terms again, and Francis sings of his reluctance to fight in wars or to work in offices. He just wishes to live his life the way he chooses (see Simichidas's song, lines 96–127, in the seventh *Idyll of Theocritus*).

The poet replies with another song, of the love of Ellen Aubrey. The friends return homeward that moonlit night, sauntering downhill to an oil-calm bay. The last ten lines of the concluding stanza are well worth study for their descriptive beauty.

the bay runs up its latest horn i.e. curves towards its promontory.

aftermath Second growth of grass for hay-cutting.

pillar'd A reference to *Paradise Lost*, Book 9, line 1106: 'Pillard shade'.

The four-field system ... till he laugh'd aloud A reference to the Corn Laws, and the terminal illness of King William IV, who died in 1837, one of the years the harvest failed.

and we were glad at heart Tennyson translated this from the *Iliad*, (Book 8, line 559) as 'the shepherd gladdens in his heart'.

The Ballad of Oriana (ME 50)

The ballad was first published in 1830 and was possibly inspired by the ballad of Helen of Kirkconnell. Oriana has its origins in the romance of *Amadis de Gaula*, a Spanish (or

Portuguese) romance by Garcia de Montalvo (late 15th century). It appears in the plays of John Fletcher (1759–1625) and in Sir Walter Scott's *Marmion* (1808): 'My heart is wasted with my woe, Oriana.' Note the welcome break in the monotonous repetition of the name 'Oriana', in the middle of each stanza, like a change of step. All lines rhyme in individual stanzas, though on occasions there is assonance, as with 'woe' and 'below', 'space' and 'brays'.

Norland A county of Norway.

The Beggar Maid (ME 264)

This is no more than the legend of a beautiful beggar maid; when the king beheld her he swore an oath: 'This beggar maid shall be my queen.' There is little substance to the poem, but is analogous to *Romeo and Juliet*, II,1,13–14: 'Young auburn Cupid, he that shot so trim/When King Cophetua loved the beggar-maid!' The lyric was written in September 1833.

mien General bearing and appearance.

The Blackbird (ME 130)

This is a simple but delightful nature poem written in 1833. It was included with six other poems in *Poems of 1842*, Vol 1 and it is noticeable that this and *Love Thou Thy Land* scan and rhyme like *In Memoriam* (*abba*), which Tennyson began writing in the same year.

The poet asks the blackbird to sing to him his most melodious song, though the neighbours treat him as a pest; he offers the bird the free run of his garden and the fruit that grows there. It sings beautifully in cold February but when the plenty of summer comes its voice becomes cacophonous, like that of a hawker shouting his wares.

There is no song during the height of summer, but early in spring he will sing for want of food: 'ere leaves are new,/Caught in the frozen palms of Spring' – a fine metaphor.

espaliers Fruit trees trained on lateral wires.
standards Fruit trees in natural vertical growth.
black-hearts Cherries.
jenneting A kind of early apple.
the silver-tongue The melodious notes of the blackbird are very noticeable early in the year.
Now thy flute-notes ... or hoarse These lines resemble two found in *Paradise Lost*, Book 8, lines 24–5: 'More safe I sing with mortal voice, unchang'd/To hoarce or mute, though fallen on evil dayes . . .'

Break, Break, Break (F 112; ME 273; OUP 132)

This poem should be read in conjunction with *In Memoriam*; it was inspired directly by the death of his friend Arthur Hallam. Hallam's body was brought home from Europe to Clevedon, Avon, where he was buried beside his maternal grandfather, Sir Abraham Elton, in the chancel of a little church overlooking the Severn estuary.

It is one of Tennyson's finest lyrics, full of pathos. We sense the melancholy of the desolate scene, the waves breaking unremittingly on the rocks at the base of the cliff. The poet is so overcome with sadness that he cannot speak. The fisherman's boy playing with his sister in the bay, and the sailor singing in his boat, are happy, but their joy only accentuates his own grief. A ship glides on about its business; life goes on and seems uncaring of his feelings and his loss.

In this poem Tennyson expresses all his tenderest love and

sorrow, heightened by the seemingly indifferent world in which life revolves: the eternal cycle of birth, life and death, ebb and flow, 'Break, break, break'. The last stanza, in particular, is a passionate cry of grief in lost love, coming straight from the heart.

The four quatrains, rhyming *abcb*, were written in a Lincolnshire country lane not far from Tennyson's birthplace and home at Somersby.

A Character (ME 42)

This satirical poem was praised highly when it first appeared in 1830. It was said to have been directed at a contemporary at Cambridge University, a student named Thomas Sunderland, whom Edward Fitzgerald described as a very plausible, parliamentary-like and self-satisfied speaker of the Union. Notwithstanding his complacency, the character was uninformed, unreceptive, dry-as-dust. His mannerism was to smooth his hair and chin. He had a lack-lustre dead-blue eye when intent on moralizing in the name of wisdom. He talked with affected delicacy for hours on the human mysteries and was completely sure of his superior knowledge.

Pallas Cognomen (family name) of the Greek mythical character, Athene. She was regarded as the goddess of Wisdom.
Juno The Roman equivalent of the Greek Hera, who was worshipped as queen of the heavens, the protectress of wives in marriage.
Devolved his rounded periods i.e. delivered his carefully constructed speeches.
trod on silk i.e. with affected delicacy and fastidiousness.

Circumstance (ME 53)

Nine lines of verse that speak of life and death; first published in 1830 and included in the 1870 *Juvenilia*. In this instance 'circumstance' has a wider meaning than usual, involving external conditions that might affect an agent. The word here conveys the same meaning in 'The Palace of Art'. Tennyson has condensed into nine lines what some writers would expand into an entire book.

Claribel (ME 19; OUP 53)

Subtitled 'A Melody'. Tennyson eventually included this among his *Juvenilia* because it first appeared as early as 1830. He comments on this, and the other vignettes of girls, by saying that all these ladies were evolved, 'like a camel, from my own consciousness'. Christopher Ricks, in his Notes to *The Poems of Tennyson*, believes that the name of this particular poem was suggested by the innocent Claribel, killed by her jealous lover in Spenser's *Faerie Queene*, 2,4,29. Note the archaic suffix '-eth'.

At eve the beetle boometh i.e. the sound of beetles which take flight just after the sun goes down.
lintwhite Linnet
mavis ... throstle Song thrushes.
crispeth Curled.
The hollow grot ... Claribel low-lieth i.e. the grotto echoes where Claribel lies.

from The Day-Dream (ME 228)

It has been suggested that the poet may have had Rosa Baring in mind when writing the legend of *The Day-Dream*. He fell in love with her in 1833 and she was possibly the model for Maud in the monodrama published in 1855. Undoubtedly Rosa had a lingering effect upon Tennyson's emotions.

There are nine sections in this poem, the first, 'The

Sleeping Princess', being written in 1830. The last to appear were the Prologue and the Epilogue. All except these two have eight-line stanzas with alternate-line rhyming. Note the 'cockney' rhyming of 'rocks' and 'fox', 'there' and 'fair', 'knee' and 'be', and the eye-rhyming of 'forth' and 'worth'. These methods of rhyming are not generally favoured by purists or by foreign students attempting to master the intricacies of English verse-construction.

This is simply the age-old fairy-tale of the sleeping princess. Here not only the princess falls asleep but everyone within the bounds of the palace: the king, his barons and servants, the birds nesting on the building. During the hundred-year sleep an impenetrable forest grows round the palace, preventing intruders from entering. At the end of the hundred years the prince arrives, kisses the princess (thereby releasing everyone from the effects of the spell) and flies off with her.

The tale is told to a fictitious Lady Flora; the poet only feels justified in telling it if he adds a moral – but he insists everyone should find his own. Each man, he is saying, should interpret beauty in Art and Nature in whatever way he chooses: beauty is in the eye of the beholder.

'Prologue' (ME 228)

damask-cheek Rose-like cheek.

dewy sister-eyelids A reference to 'To Rosa', 2,10: 'And dewy sister eyelids drooping chaste . . .'

A summer crisp with shining woods See 'The Gardener's Daughter' (ME 154) lines 29–31.

Macaw A parrot.

'The Sleeping Palace' (ME 229)

Oriel Projecting window of upper storey.

woodbine Honeysuckle.

'The Arrival' (ME 232)

thorny close Prickly enclosure.

More close and close Closer and closer. Written, no doubt, for the sake of scansion, and to express a certain caution.

quick and quicker Faster and faster, in contrast to the pace of his physical approach. The Magic Music in his heart speeds up steadily.

'L'Envoi' (ME 236)

decads Decades.

quinquenniads Five-yearly periods.

For since the time when Adam first Genesis, 2,23: And Adam said, This is now bone of my bones, and flesh of my flesh: she shall be called Woman, because she was taken out of Man.

'Epilogue' (ME 238)

birds of Paradise A New Guinea species of bird, brightly-coloured and with long, flowing tail in flight.

The Death of the Old Year (ME 131)

First published in 1832, the poem personifies the Old Year as a dying old man awaiting the New Year. At this time Arthur Hallam was courting Tennyson's sister Emily. The two men had toured the Rhine but had difficulties over quarantine in Holland and were delayed for some time. When in England Hallam, who was then studying Law, was a frequent visitor to Somersby, and hoped to marry Emily in the coming year. The poet is referring to the domestic situation in the lines 'He gave me a friend, and a true true-love,/And the New-year will take 'em away.' A reference, no doubt, to their forthcoming marriage; he is loath to see the old year go because of the happiness it has brought them – and he had no knowledge of the tragedy to come.

A Dirge (ME 47)

First published in 1830, the lilt of this poem is reminiscent of Shakespeare's *Cymbeline*, IV,2,258: 'Fear no more the heat o' the sun . . .'

birk Northern expression for birch.
carketh i.e. vexeth.
eglatere (Usually spelt 'eglantine'); Sweet-briar.
pleached Entwined, interlaced.
long purples i.e. the purple vetch, a climbing plant.
balm-cricket i.e. the cicada, an insect remarkable for its chirping sound.

Dora (ME 163)

There is a Wordsworthian simplicity in the language of this idyll written in 1835, and its style resembles 'Michael', Wordsworth's poem which Tennyson had read to Fitzgerald that same year. The story, rather melodramatic, is based on Mary Russell Mitford's 'Dora Creswell'. It appears in the book *Our Village* (1828), which depicts the villagers of Three Mile Cross, Berkshire. The poet's reading of 'Michael' must have been fresh in his mind because he even used the Christian names of Wordsworth, his wife Mary, and daughter Dora, who married Edward Quillinan.

In 'Dora' the scene is set on a farm, the farmer being Allan, his son William and Dora, his niece. The farmer plans to marry off William to Dora, but his son has other notions. However, Dora herself is willing to marry William to please her uncle.

William leaves home, his father's warning not to return

ringing in his ears. William marries Mary Morrison, a labourer's daughter, half in love, half in spite. They have a boy, but William sickens and dies. Secretly Dora supports Mary and the boy, because Mary is too poor to manage on her own. They meet, plan to induce Dora's uncle to accept the boy, which he does unwillingly.

Eventually farmer Allan relents, and Dora, Mary, the child and the farmer live together in the same house. Mary marries again, but Dora remains a spinster till her death. Is it mere coincidence that Wordsworth's sister, Dorothy, remained a spinster in the poet's house all her life, though he married Mary Hutchinson?

It is interesting to note the poet's comments on the composition of this poem, in Hallam Tennyson's *Memoir*: ' "Dora" . . . the tale of a simple country girl, had to be told in the simplest possible poetical language, and was therefore one of the poems which gave most trouble.' This, perhaps more than any other poem, caused Tennyson to appreciate the great art underlying Wordsworth's apparently simple lyrical ballads.

A Dream of Fair Women (ME 118)

This poem was published in 1832. Tennyson said of line 3, 'Chaucer, the first great English poet, wrote *The Legend of Good Women*. From among these Cleopatra alone appears in my poem.' Hallam Tennyson's *Memoir* discloses that in the first edition the poet begins with some stanzas about a man sailing in a balloon; Tennyson decided he did not like these stanzas, so they were omitted.

The poet falls asleep reading *The Legend of Good Women*, and the images of famous 'good women' pass in succession through his subconscious mind. The first he meets is 'A daughter of the gods, divinely tall,/And most divinely fair.' She is Helen, daughter of Zeus and Leda.

The second fair woman is Cleopatra, who haughtily asks for Mark Antony, her lover, who died in her bosom. Next he encounters the daughter of the warrior Gileadite in Israel, who died for God and her sire. Leaving him, she sings 'Glory to God'. She is replaced by Rosamund de Clifford, Henry II's mistress, who was poisoned by Queen Eleanor. The 'captain' referred to here is Venus, the star of morning.

Tennyson once said that lines 265–7 refer to Margaret Roper, Sir Thomas More's daughter, who is supposed to have taken her father's head from the Tower of London to be buried in a church in Chelsea. The head had been on public display for fourteen days and was soon to be thrown into the Thames to make way for other poor beheaded mortals. Margaret had actually bought the head, taken it and climbed into a coffin with it, where eventually she was found.

The dreamer sees next the image of Eleanor, wife of Edward I. When the dream ends the poet wishes that it could be repeated, but knows no two dreams can be the same.

morning star of song So named by Arthur Hallam.

Dan Chaucer A reference to Spenser's *Faerie Queene*, 4,2, stanza 32: 'Dan Chaucer, well of English undefyled.'

the hollow dark A reference to Keats's posthumously published *The Fall of Hyperion*, 1,455: 'And stretched her white arm through the hollow dark.'

tortoise Christopher Ricks describes this as the 'testudo' of ancient war, in which warriors advanced towards a wall with shields above their heads.

seraglios i.e. the harems enclosed by the walls of ancient palaces.

The dim red morn had died Tennyson explains it as referring to the early past. 'How magnificently old Turner would have painted it!'

the end of time Revelation, 10,6: '. . . that there should be time no longer.'

My father held his hand upon his face Hallam Tennyson
comments: 'My father had in his mind the famous picture by
Timanthes, the *Sacrifice of Iphigeneia* . . . of which there is a
Pompeiian wall-painting.'

Whereto the other . . . Then when I left my home See *Iliad*,
6,345: 'I would that on the day when first my mother gave me
birth an evil storm-wind had borne me away to some mountain
or to the wave of the loud-resounding sea, where the wave
might have swept me away or ever these things came to pass.'

A queen, with swarthy cheeks See Shakespeare's *Antony and
Cleopatra*, I,5,27: 'Think of me/That am with Phoebus' amorous
pinches black.'

Brow-bound with burning gold See Shakespeare's *Coriolanus*,
II,2,103: 'brow-bound with the oak'.

Canopus In the constellation of Argo.

I died a queen . . . Worthy a Roman spouse A reference to
Cleopatra's death in Horace's *Odes*, 1,37,32.

The daughter of the warrior Gileadite A reference to Judges
11,34: 'And Jephthah came to Mizpeh unto his house, and,
behold, his daughter came up to meet him with timbrels and
with dances: and she was *his* only child; beside her he had
neither son nor daughter.'

a threefold cord See Ecclesiastes, 4,12: 'and a threefold cord is
not quickly broken.'

the everlasting hills See Genesis, 49,26: 'The blessings of thy
father have prevailed above the blessings of my progenitors
unto the utmost bound of the everlasting hills.'

Thridding the sombre boskage of the wood i.e. slipping
through the dark thickets.

her who knew that Love can vanquish Death A reference to
Eleanor, the wife of Edward I. She accompanied him to the
Holy Land in 1269; while at Acre Edward was stabbed with a
poisoned dagger and Eleanor sucked the poison from his
wound.

cull'd Chosen, picked out.

The Dying Swan (ME 46; OUP 57)

There is a legend that a wild swan sings its own coronach or death-hymn, and this is the theme of 'The Dying Swan', first published in 1832 and included in the *Juvenilia*.

The poet paints a haunting picture of a wide, bare plain, and through it at midday is seen flowing a marshy river bordered by reeds. In it floats the dying swan singing its coronach as the weary wind sighs through the waving reed-tops.

There are distant blue mountains crowned by shining white snowy peaks; a willow weeps; a swallow cavorts in the air chasing flies; the tangled, marshy watercourses sleep in silence and without motion; and over them are splashes of colour – purple, green and yellow.

Soon the dying swan begins to warble, barely audibly, its tone sometimes heard far, sometimes near. But soon its voice, 'with a music strange and manifold' is heard. The poem ends with a delightful descriptive passage that should be studied for onomatopoeic effects and vivid epithets: 'creeping mosses' and 'clambering weeds'; 'willow-branches hoar and dank'; 'wavy swell of the soughing reeds'; 'wave-worn horns' of the 'echoing bank'.

marish Marshy.
coronach Death-song.
shawms Obsolete instruments with a double reed.
soughing Poetical variation of sighing.

Edward Gray (ME 246)

Tennyson wrote this poem in the year of his broken engagement to Emily Sellwood (1840). For ten more years the couple were forbidden by Emily's parents to meet. This poem, and 'Love and Duty', speak volumes on the poet's heartbreak. He called 'Edward Gray' a virgin-ballad, and it was one of the *English Idylls* published in 1842. Tennyson may have borrowed the name Edward Gray from Mary Russell Mitford's 'The Queen of the Meadow' in *Our Village* (1827).

Eleänore (ME 66)

This poem, addressed to Eleänore in gay euphoric language, with a plethora of vivid epithets, was written in 1832 at the height of Tennyson's friendship with Arthur Hallam. The cosseted luxury of Eleänore's upbringing is shown; she has swan-like stateliness and grace. In her, all passion loses its fire, and the spirit mellows. Love can but languidly regard the serene, imperial Eleänore. While in a charmed slumber, the poet suddenly feels a languid fire creep through his veins: Eleänore pronounces his name. He dies, 'Brimm'd with delirious draughts of warmest life', with his delight, before he hears what he would from her – his name.

cull'd Extracted.
salvers Trays of silver, gold or brass.
lineament Distinctive feature.
censer A vessel for burning incense.
ambrosial Heavenly, god-like.
tresses Hair.

The Epic (ME 143)

Edward Fitzgerald recorded that 'The Epic' was written after 1835, and Christopher Ricks, in his Notes on *The Poems of 1842*, estimates that it was some time between 1837/8. Fitzgerald comments that it was an attempt 'to anticipate or excuse the "faint Homeric echoes", etc. (as in 'The Day-Dream') to give a reason for telling an old-world tale' (see Hallam Tennyson's *Memoir*, vol. 1).

In 'The Epic' Tennyson fleshed out the body, though somewhat ethereally, of the King Arthur of *Morte d'Arthur*, which was written as a direct result of Arthur Hallam's death. A trial version of *Morte d'Arthur* in 1842, lacked the prefatory 'Epic', but it was included in the two-volume edition published that year.

At a Christmas gathering attended by the poet and old Cambridge friends, the conversation eventually turns from the subject of the decline in the festivities and Christian faith generally, to the subject of the poet's work . . . What had become of his verse since leaving university? A friend discloses that he had written an epic of some twelve books on King Arthur, but burned them. But why? the others ask. He had nothing new to say on the topic. 'The truth looks freshest in the fashion of the day'; why not remodel them? But, no, he's adamant:

> . . . these twelve books of mine
> Were faint Homeric echoes, nothing-worth,
> Mere chaff and draff, much better burnt.

But Frank admits to having rescued the penultimate book from the flames – 'keep a thing, its use will come./I hoard it as a sugar-plum for Holmes.' Everard takes the book from him and reads just as Tennyson himself would read: '. . . mouthing out his hollow *o*s and *a*s,/Deep-chested music, and to this result.' [Then followed *Morte d'Arthur*.]

wassail-bowl Drinking-bowl.

cutting eights that day upon the pond The poet often used to skate on the frozen lake at Epping Park after the Tennysons moved to High Beech in 1837.

church-commissioners A reference to the Ecclesiastical Commissioners Act of 1836, revised in 1840/1.

Geology and schism Geology was a threat to Christian doctrine even before the evolutionary theories of Charles Darwin were published in *The Origin of Species* (1859).

no anchor The foundations of Christianity had been eroded.

Mastodon Extinct gargantuan mammal.

Were faint Homeric echoes A reference to Edward
Fitzgerald's criticism of *The Epic*; see above.

pick'd the eleventh from this hearth There is a story that
after criticism of his early work on the *Idylls*, the poet burned a
set of twelve books on King Arthur's legend, but that a friend
saved the last of the series, not the penultimate as indicated
here.

Read, mouthing . . . and to this result Describes Tennyson's
own manner of verse-reading.

A Farewell (F 111; ME 263)

Another delightful lyric in which rhyme schemes overlap
cleverly through the four stanzas: first and third lines, 'sea,
be', 'lea, be', 'tree, bee', 'thee, be'; the second lines, 'deliver,
river, shiver, quiver'; and the fourth line is the same in each
– 'For ever and for ever', euphoniously blending the *ever* with
the second-line '-*ivers*'. Moreover there is alliteration throughout with the placement of vowels and consonants to evoke
sound and mood and stimulate sensations.

In the first stanza we have the rivulet emerging from the
spring, 'Flow down, cold rivulet, to the sea', and he bids it
farewell. He remembers in the second how it broadens from
a stream to a river, its pace slowing – 'Flow, softly flow' –
between lawn and lea, until he hears the sigh of the alder
and sees the aspen shiver. He hears the humming bee, and
reflects that a thousand suns and moons will shine and
quiver as they are reflected in its waters, but unseen by him –
'For ever and for ever'.

Tennyson, as in so many of his songs and lyrics, blends a
vivid imagination with remarkable poetical technique, at the
same time remembering to be meticulous in the matter of
recording correctly the minutiae of Nature.

'A Farewell' was composed in 1837 on the departure of the Tennyson family from Somersby Rectory, Lincolnshire and was addressed to the Somersby Brook.

Fatima (ME 79; OUP 58)

First published in 1832 (lines 8–14 were added for the 1842 edition) this poem, in common with 'The Vision of Sin', 'Love and Duty' and *Maud*, reveals the degree of Tennyson's passion for Rosa Baring, and the extent of his sexuality, which he was apparently able to sublimate until his marriage in 1850 at the age of forty-one. Unlike Swinburne, whose one great passion for his first cousin, Mary Gordon, was never gratified, and who, as a result, nearly drank himself to death, Tennyson had a strong sense of duty and self-control. However, the combination of losing Rosa, and the death of his friend in the following year, sorely tried him. It was many years before he regained his faith and overcame bitterness.

So here, to disguise his true feelings, his emotions are expressed by Fatima. This is one of Tennyson's most sensual poems, comparable with many in Swinburne's *Poems and Ballads: First Series* (1866). Note, for example, the following stanza lines: 'A thousand little shafts of flame/Were shivered in my narrow frame./O Love, O fire! once he drew/With one long kiss my whole soul thro'/My lips, as sunlight drinketh dew.'

Notice that the first four lines of each stanza rhyme as well as the last three. Note also in the next stanza the onomatopoeic effects of the sibilants, the warm vowels and tonality.

athwart Across.
drouth Drought.

The Gardener's Daughter (ME 154)

'The Gardener's Daughter: or The Pictures' is the full title of this poem, first published in 1842; but actually written in 1833–4. According to Hallam Tennyson's *Memoir*, the poet remarked that it united Arthur Hallam's love for Tennyson's sister Emily, with his own love for Rosa Baring. In the narrative Eustace is Hallam, and Juliet is his sister Emily, while his love is for Rose, or Rosa.

The extent of Arthur Hallam's feeling for the poet is expressed in a letter sent to him in Scotland (31 July 1833): 'I feel tonight what I own has been too uncommon with me of late, a strong desire to write to you . . . I missed you much at Somersby – not for want of additional excitement, I was very happy . . . I trust you finished *The Gardener's Daughter* and enriched her with a few additional beauties drawn from the ancient countenance of Monteith's aunt. Have you encountered any Highland girl with "a shower for her dower"?'

Elsewhere in *Memoir*, Hallam Tennyson quotes his father as saying of this poem: 'The centre of the poem, that passage describing the girl, must be full and rich. The poem is so, to a fault, especially the description of nature, for the lover is an artist, but, this being so, the central picture must hold its place.' Not only are the lovers artists, but the poet infers also that true love inspires the finest art.

Rosa Baring was the step-daughter of Admiral Eden and they lived at Harrington Hall, a delightful Queen Anne house about two miles from Somersby. Note, therefore, the reference to Eden in the text – 'Henceforward squall nor storm/Could keep me from that Eden where she dwelt'.

Although they loved each other, Rosa eventually turned the poet down, and married Robert Shafto (for money) in 1838. Nevertheless, Tennyson remembered her to the end, and in 1889, in *Demeter* wrote some lines to her in 'The Roses on the Terrace': 'Rose, on this terrace fifty years ago,/When I was in my June, you in your May,/Two words, "*My* Rose" set all your face aglow,/And now that I am white, and you are grey . . .'

In the poem Rose accepts the artist's proposal of marriage; whether Rosa accepted him is another matter. The final lines, 269–73, carry perhaps more truth in real life than he would admit. Lines 26–8 are descriptive of his sister Emily.

The lime a summer home of murmurous wings A delightful onomatopoeic line, recalling the editor's visit to Somersby church, when the fragrance of the limes' fallen winged seeds strongly pervaded the air.

ouzel A kind of small water bird.

Hebe Goddess of Youth.

Titianic Flora A painting by Titian (1477–1576), in Florence.

Eden Literally, a delightful abode, but here Tennyson refers to Admiral Eden, Rosa Baring's step-father.

Godiva (ME 209)

Written in 1840, 'Godiva' was published in 1842 to commemorate the poet's visit to Coventry. Emerson wrote that he considered it a noble poem that would tell the legend a thousand years. However, Leigh Hunt took a less favourable view of this poem and 'Morte D'Arthur', complaining of:

. . . a certain air of literary dandyism, or fine-gentlemanism, or fastidiousness, or whatever he may not be pleased to call it, which leads him to usher in his compositions with such exordiums as those to 'Morte d'Arthur', and 'Godiva'; in the former of which he gives us to understand that he should have burnt his poem [see *The Epic*] but for the 'request of friends'; and in the latter, that he 'shaped' it while he was waiting 'for the train at Coventry', and hanging on the Bridge 'with grooms and porters' . . . We suspect that these poems of 'Morte d'Arthur' and 'Godiva' are among those which Mr Tennyson thinks his best . . . and therefore it is that he would affect to make trifles of them. The reader's opinion is at once to be of great importance to him, and yet none at all.

The poem is in iambic pentameters of blank verse, with the four-line introduction which peeved Leigh Hunt so sorely.

Godiva The wife of Leofric, earl of Mercia, one of Edward the Confessor's great earls. According to legend, her husband having imposed a tax on the inhabitants of Coventry, she begged him to remit it, which he jestingly promised to do if she would ride naked through the streets at noonday. Lady Godiva took him at his word, directed the people to keep within doors and shut their windows, and complied with his condition. Peeping Tom, who looked out, was struck blind. The story is told by Drayton in *Polyolbion*; by Leigh Hunt himself; and she appears as Hereward's mother in *Hereward the Wake* by Charles Kingsley. Godiva also appears in Landor's *Imaginary Conversations*.

rough as Esau's hand See Genesis, 27,23: '. . . his hands were hairy, as his brother Esau's hands.'

palfrey Saddle-horse for ladies.

churl Boor or ill-bred fellow.

The Goose (ME 141)

Though only a fable, 'The Goose' can be bracketed with two other political poems in the 1842 collection: 'Of old sat Freedom on the Heights', and 'Love Thou Thy Land, with Love Far-Brought'. It was written just after the Reform Bill was passed in Parliament, causing some public disturbance. It is composed in a jingle of alternate-rhyming lines in quatrains. The moral is inescapable.

pelf i.e. booty.

Isabel (ME 21)

This woman's eyes reveal innocence 'fed with the clear-pointed flame of chastity . . .' She is pure of spirit, a perfect, self-effacing creature, but with intelligence – indeed, the ideal wife; here the poet is describing his mother. In the poem there are references to Belphoebe in Spenser's *Faerie Queene*, Shelley's Dedication to the *Revolt of Islam* and Thomas Heywood's *A Woman killed with Kindness*.

fane Temple.
parlance A manner of speaking.

Lady Clara Vere de Vere (ME 101)

Another portrait of a woman to fill the poet's gallery. Lady Clara Vere de Vere, taking advantage of her great wealth and estates, attempts to ensnare the emotions of one whom she takes to be a simple countryman. But the fellow is wise to her wiles and is on his guard. She is undesirable to him because of her aristocratic pride and her known delight in inflicting emotional wounds for the pleasure of it. The country fellow loves a simple maiden, worth a hundred of Lady Clara's sort; he knows the rumours concerning the death of her late husband, a mysterious, violent death. Her mother had told her, in no uncertain terms, just what she thought of her: 'And slew him with your noble birth . . . Kind hearts are more than coronets,/And simple faith than Norman blood.'

  The poem was written in 1835, at about the same time as its successor, 'Lady Clare'. When it was published in 1842 Tennyson described it as a dramatic poem drawn from no particular character.

The gardener Adam and his wife A reference to Adam in
  the Garden of Eden.

Lady Clare (ME 256)

This poem is based on a novel, *The Inheritance*, by Susan
Ferrier (1752–1854). Lord Ronald courts his cousin Lady
Clare, and they are to be married the next day. But then her
nurse Alice reveals a secret: Clare is not really the dead earl's
child and will not inherit wealth and the estates as she had
always been led to believe. In fact the little girl who *was* to
inherit the estates died young, and Alice had been induced
to replace her with her own daughter Clare.

Alice begs her to go through with the marriage and to
keep her own counsel, but Clare insists on testing Lord
Ronald's love by disclosing the secret. If he really loves her
the truth will not matter; if he refuses to go through with the
marriage she will know he had merely sought her wealth.
She comes to him dressed as a simple country girl. His
curiosity aroused, she then proceeds to tell him Alice's story.
Nothing daunted, he still insists on marrying her: he will
inherit the estates instead, and no harm has been done.

The Lady of Shalott (F 79; ME 57; OUP 60)

The first version of this poem was written and published in
1832, but was criticized as being too ornamental. It was
based broadly on the Italian novelette *Donna di Scolatta*. Ten
years passed before the drastically revised version – a great
improvement on the original – was published in the 1842
volumes. Where the first was lavishly descriptive, the second
version achieved beauty in its simplicity of diction and
description.

It is a tale of magic symbolism with deep human significance, in which 'the fairy Lady of Shalott' is bound by a spell
to remain for ever in her room in the castle of Camelot. She
weaves ceaselessly at her loom, and knows that she must

never gaze directly on the world outside, but only through her mirror. She beholds its beauties only as images – a theme analogous to the Soul in Tennyson's 'Palace of Art', but in which the world is deliberately excluded and the Soul feeds on the delights of the world's greatest Art. If the Lady of Shalott were to see the world as reality, the spell would be broken and death would follow automatically.

Inevitably this happens when, in Part 3, Sir Lancelot appears on the scene garbed in his glistening armour and finery. The image of him draws her irresistibly to the window, for though she lacks nothing material in life, she has never known love. The attraction of love is stronger than her fear of death, and as she looks on her knight the spell is broken. But she does not regret the moment of delight when love awakens in her breast.

The Lady of Shalott prepares herself to die and goes down to the banks of the river. She writes her name on the prow of the boat, drifts downstream, singing sadly; soon she dies. When her boat comes to rest at the wharf at Camelot the sight of her strikes fear and awe into every knight save Sir Lancelot who, gazing at her, says: 'She has a lovely face;/God in his mercy lend her grace.' Hallam Tennyson says that the key to the poem is in lines 69–72. A companion poem to this was 'Life of the Life within my Blood', which was not, however, published during the poet's lifetime.

Commenting on 'The Lady of Shalott', Tennyson said that his version of the fairy-tale was different from the original in *Donna di Scalotta*: 'but the web, mirror, island etc. were my own. Indeed I doubt whether I should ever have put it in that shape if I had been then aware of the Maid of Astolat in *Morte d'Arthur* (Malory).' The Lady of Shalott becomes Elaine in Tennyson's 'Morte d'Arthur', which in turn becomes 'Lancelot and Elaine' in his later versions. The poet preferred the softer-sounding 'Shalott' to the original

'Scalotta'; the name is derived not only from 'Scalotta', but also from *Astolat*, *Ascolat* or *Escalot* (see Malory's *Morte d'Arthur*, Book 18, 9–20).

The rhyming pattern of the poem is *aaaabcccb* but the octosyllabic metre is not consistent throughout (see, for example, lines 7 and 8 in the first stanza.)

Camelot Malory claims that it was situated at Winchester, others believe it was at Guildford. It is, however, generally accepted that Camelot Castle was on the site of the existing Cadbury Castle, between Queen Camel and South Cadbury, near the A303 road.

aspens Trees whose leaves quiver.

shallop Light, open boat.

I am half sick of shadows The Lady of Shalott's most revealing thought. She, who has no knight of her own, is bitterly envious of the young lovers in their newly-wedded delight.

greaves Pieces of armour to guard the shins.

gemmy Gem-adorned or encrusted.

baldric Belt for sword or musical instrument hung diagonally from one shoulder to the opposite hip.

bearded meteor Falling meteor with a trail of burning particles.

His broad clean brow ... His coal-black curls The emphasis throughout Part 3 is on Lancelot's tremendous physical attraction.

She left the web ... thro' the room Fine illustration of the swiftness with which she succumbs to the lure of Lancelot – even the spell is forgotten.

prow The bow.

seer Prophet.

snowy white ... singing her last song Marvellous swan imagery; Ophelia, too, sang before she died: 'Which time she chanted snatches of old tunes/As one incapable of her own distress.' (*Hamlet*, IV,7,178–9).

burgher Here, a townsman.

Locksley Hall (ME 196; OUP 93)

The hero revisits his childhood home, recalling his love for his cousin Amy, a 'shallow-hearted' creature, who abandoned him in deference to her parents for a worldly marriage. This evokes a bitter tirade against her weakness, and a stream of sarcastic 'advice' as to how she should treat her 'clown': 'Go to him: it is thy duty: kiss him: take his hand in thine.' He rails against a society that keeps young lovers apart for reasons of respectability and money and prevents them being true to themselves.

He prophesies a future of thriving commerce and horrifying wars; his fantasy takes him to the refuge of a paradise isle and a life close to Nature; but he decides, in the end, that there is still cause for optimism in Europe, and turns his back on the past.

Tennyson claimed that 'Locksley Hall' was a figment of his imagination, but he certainly set the scene on the Lincolnshire coast, probably near Mablethorpe, where his family spent their holidays. Locksley Hall is generally identified with Harrington Hall, two miles from Somersby. Whatever Tennyson may have claimed concerning the poem's origins, there is little doubt that Amy is the counterpart of Rosa Baring.

The late Sir Charles Tennyson, grandson of the poet, put forward his own views on the poem's origins, maintaining that the episode at Locksley Hall is based on the differences and bitterness that existed between the two branches of the Tennyson family. It was the poverty of the Somersby branch of the Tennyson family that was the true cause of Rosa Baring's rejection of his love.

Once Tennyson heard the following story: two undergraduates were walking together some time after he himself had left Cambridge. One of the two mentioned 'Tennyson'.

The other replied 'O do not mention that man's name. I hate him. I was the unhappy hero of "Locksley Hall". It is the story of my cousin's love and mine, known to all Cambridge when Tennyson was there, and he put it into verse.' Tennyson had never, in fact, heard of either the undergraduate or his unhappy love.

ivied casement Ivy-surrounded window-frame.

Orion One of the constellations containing seven bright stars, three of which, in a straight line, form Orion's 'belt', the remainder his 'sword'.

Pleiads From the *Moâllakát*: 'It was the hour when the Pleiads appeared in the firmament.' Hallam Tennyson says in his *Memoir*: 'I remember my father saying that Sir William Jones's prose translation of the *Moâllakát*, the seven Arabic poems (which are a selection from the work of pre-Mahommedan poets) hanging up in the temple of Mecca, gave him the idea of the poem.'

glowing hands See *The Eve of St Agnes* (John Keats, 1795–1821): 'These delicates he heap'd with glowing hand/On golden dishes and in baskets bright' (31,271–2).

thou art mated with a clown The poet's contemptuous view of Robert Shafto.

As the many-winter'd crow Rooks are called crows in the northern counties.

For I dipt into the future From this point he looks ahead to wars, the state of the world, trade, government.

argosies Large merchant vessels, richly laden.

Pilots ... bales Traders ... wares.

palsied i.e. drained of energy, powerless.

wroth Wrathful.

Mahratta Member of a warlike, Hindi-speaking Indian race.

There the passions cramp'd i.e. in the name of respectability.

Joshua's moon in Ajalon See Joshua, 10,12. 'Sun, stand thou still upon Gibeon; and thou, Moon, in the valley of Ajalon.'

Let the great world spin Tennyson's own explanation: 'When I went by the first train from Liverpool to Manchester (1830), I thought that the wheels ran in a groove. It was a black night and there was such a vast crowd round the train at the station that we could not see the wheels. Then I made this line.'

Cathay China.

Rift Here a verb, meaning to split open.

crescent i.e. increasing, ever growing.

vapour from the margin i.e. black cloud from the horizon.

holt Wood.

Lilian (ME 20)

Lilian is a flirty, coquettish young lady of somewhat superficial character. The poem was first published in 1830. Leigh Hunt criticized what he termed the injudicious crowding of images 'which sometimes results from Mr Tennyson's desire to impress upon us the abundance of his thoughts.' He had in mind particularly lines 16 and 17 in the second stanza. The poet was very fond, at that time, of using hyphenated epithets, and he certainly uses them to effect throughout this poem: 'love-sighs', 'black-beaded', 'baby-roses', 'silver-treble' – all illustrate his gift as a word-painter.

wimple Cloth worn over the head.

Prythee weep Much of Tennyson's early poetry employs archaic words. The intention may be to date the period to earlier times.

When from crimson-threaded lips See Song of Solomon, 4,3: 'Your lips are like a scarlet thread'.

The Lord of Burleigh (ME 259)

The story of a country girl who marries a landscape-painter. They tour various manorial estates until they arrive at the finest of them all, which proves to be his – for he is the Lord of Burleigh. The girl tries to adapt herself to the new situation and, on the face of it, succeeds admirably: 'And her gentle mind was such/That she grew a noble lady,/And the people loved her much.' She bears him three children, grows daily weaker, and dies young, crushed by the burden of the high rank to which she was not born. The once simple country girl is buried in her wedding dress 'that her spirit might have rest.'

The story is based on the marriage of Henry, Marquess of Exeter (1754–1804) who, in 1791, married Sarah Hoggins, of Bolas in Shropshire. The ballad was written in 1833–4. Tennyson points out that the mood changes from happiness to sadness in lines 63–4, and at the same time the tense changes from present to past.

The Lotos-Eaters (F 85; ME 112; OUP 75)

Ulysses, the king of Ithaca, a small island in the Ionian Sea, is returning home with his men from the Trojan war. The episode of the lotos-eaters is retailed in Homer's *Odyssey*, Book 9. ('Lotos' is the Greek spelling of the modern 'lotus'.) The Trojan war lasted ten years. In Homer's *Iliad* Troy was the capital of Priam's kingdom, where Helen was held captive by Menelaus, king of Sparta, after she was abducted by Paris, the son of Priam.

Having successfully concluded the war, Ulysses sails with his crew. They come first to Cicones, where they obtain jars of sweet wine. Then, journeying southward, they eventually beach on the Libyan promontory of Lotophagi, the country of the lotos-eaters.

It is at the moment of their beaching that Tennyson begins his poem. In Book 9 of the *Odyssey*, the natives offer members of Ulysses's crew fruit from the locally grown lotos plant; its effect is to kill all desire to continue the voyage home to Ithaca. It induces in them a feeling of languid distaste for active life, with sensations of luxurious dreaminess. Like Epicureans, they seek only a life of leisure, ease and comfort. Their families at home no longer concern them; they are drugged.

In Homer's version of the voyage, Ulysses has to speak severely to his crew, and once aboard he punishes them. But not so in Tennyson's version, as will be seen in the 'Choric Song'.

The classical scenery which Tennyson describes is partially based on landscapes seen during his journey through the Pyrenees with Arthur Hallam in 1832; the waterfall described is the waterfall at Gavarnie.

Edmund Spenser's *Faerie Queene* primarily influenced style and metre and the formation of stanzas in this poem, though it is Homer's work on which it is based. A good deal of it is also derived from Washington Irving's *Columbus* (1842). Indeed, there is much of the spirit of Columbus in Tennyson's 'Ulysses'.

Tennyson, the word-painter, is at his finest in descriptions of natural scenery: the moonlit vale beyond the languid strand; the slender stream falling from cliffs like 'downward smoke'; a land of streams with 'slow-dropping veils of thinnest lawn' breaking through light and shadow to join the river in its course to the sea.

languid air did swoon So hot as to be enervating.
lawn Thin, almost transparent, white linen; such was the appearance of the waterfall.
Up-clomb Climbed.
galingale An aromatic East Indian plant, formerly used in medicine and cookery.
keel A low flat-bottomed boat.
mild-eyed melancholy Lotos-eaters i.e. uninterested, apathetic.
Our island home i.e. Ithaca.

from The Lotos-Eaters

'Choric Song' (F 85; ME 113; OUP 75)

The Choric Song of the Lotos-eaters expresses the Epicurean attitude to life. As in odes, stanza forms vary in length. The first stanza rhymes *ababcccdddd*, the second *aaabcbbccdcdc*. These variations and the extensive use of alliteration in rhythmical measure convey excellently the ennui, the *laissez-faire* outlook of Ulysses's crew.

In the second stanza the sailors question why they should continue their odyssey. They never have a chance to rest from it, to cease from wandering, to sleep, or to listen to what the inner spirit sings.

The lotos-eaters remember their wives with tears. But now, after ten years, their hearths will be cold; their sons will have taken over their inheritance: to return home would only disrupt the peace and joy of family life. Their great deeds at Troy now half-forgotten, why bother to leave this delightful country, where Nature provides beauty, tranquillity and plenty? They will wander no more. (The opposite view is expressed in Tennyson's 'Ulysses', lines 56–70.)

All things have rest i.e. all things in nature.
amaranth An imaginary flower that blooms perpetually.
moly A fabulous herb with a white flower and black root, endowed with magical properties.
acanthus Prickly-leaved plant, often seen sculpted in Greek architecture.
Elysian Of Elysium, a mythical abode of the blessed after death.
asphodel A kind of lily; in Greek mythology, particularly the plant of the dead.

Love and Death (ME 49)

These fifteen lines of verse were published in 1830 when

Tennyson was 21. Love wanders through Paradise in the light of the moon and encounters Death, who claims that these walks are his. Love, weeping, prepares to flee, but contends that the hour is his, for Death is the shadow of life. Love is life's tree which creates that shadow: 'So in the light of great eternity/Life eminent creates the shade of death;/The shadow passeth when the tree shall fall,/But I shall reign for ever over all.' Remarkable lines, for one so young.

lustrous eyes See Keats's 'Ode to a Nightingale', lines 29–30.
thymy Of the thyme: a herb grown in domestic kitchen-gardens, and used in cooking.
cassia Laurel.
shenny vans Gleaming wings, a phrase which may have been suggested by Milton's *Paradise Regained*, Book 4, line 583.
Life eminent Defined by the poet as meaning 'standing out like a tree.' (*Paradise Lost*, Book 4, line 219).

Love and Duty (ME 191)

In 1840 Tennyson was still desperately poor; so when Emily Sellwood's father wrote to Alfred Tennyson saying that he must no longer correspond with his daughter, Alfred's mother offered to share part of her annuity with him, but he declined. He, with a peculiar stubbornness or sense of duty, also refused to lift a finger to help himself by selling poems to journals. As a result it was mutually agreed to break off the engagement between them. In the fight between Love and Duty, Love capitulated. Robert Browning and Elizabeth Barrett showed far more courage in their determination to marry in spite of Elizabeth's illness and Robert's poverty.

Perhaps Tennyson had an over developed sense of duty because he was responsible for his branch of the family. He had already lost Rosa Baring to another: was it now to be the same with Emily? The answer to his problem lies concealed in this poem which he made sure to include with the 1842 volumes so that Emily could read it and understand his motives. They little dreamt that their marriage lay ten years away.

It should be remembered that he was, in 1840, suffering from severe depression, a neurosis aggravated by this very trouble with the Sellwoods. He was still being hounded by the critics. He had faith in the future, but poverty was a constant source of worry.

Better the narrow brain ... and apathetic end Tennyson visited Dr Allen's Fairmead Asylum, near High Beech, Epping, to see the poet John Clare, who was being treated there.

the summer night, that paused ... but the end had come See Wordsworth's 'Vandracour and Julia', 97–101: 'Meanwhile the galaxy displayed/Her fires, that like mysterious pulses beat/Aloft; – momentous but uneasy bliss/To their full hearts the universe seemed hung/On the brief meeting's slender filament!'

Live happy An echo of Milton's *Paradise Lost*, Book 8, line 633: 'Be strong, live happie, and love . . .'

mounded rack Driving clouds. See Shakespeare's *Sonnets*, No.33: 'With ugly rack on his celestial face . . .'

'Love Thou Thy Land, With Love Far-Brought'
(ME 138)

This is one of a trio of political poems written in about 1833; the other two being 'Of Old Sat Freedom on the Heights' and 'You Ask me why, Though Ill at Ease'. They were inspired by the passing of the Reform Bill of 1832. The poem, 'The Goose', also refers to the Bill, but is more of a jingle.

Stanza one encapsulates the poet's poetical ideals involving love of his homeland, to be found in many of his allegorical works, especially in *The Idylls of the King*. In the fourth stanza here, he implies that great work is not for the weak, and that love and freedom must not be withheld from those seeking it. He continues by saying that knowledge should be spread to all men equally with Reverence in the van. Take heed of events and where possible dispel prejudice with gentleness, but be wary of those in power. Do not be hasty for changes and new laws for their own sake, or too slow to accept them. The poem continues in this didactic tone throughout, showing that Tennyson was very much aware of current political events, and was even prepared to use his art to try to save his readers from falling into the pitfalls encountered by the politically naïve. His use of imagery and imagination saves the poem from becoming a political tract or sermon.

lime i.e. snare a bird with quick-lime.

Make knowledge circle ... growth of minds See the Prologue to *In Memoriam* (fifth stanza): 'Let knowledge grow from more to more,/But more of reverence in us dwell;/That mind and soul, according well,/May make one music as before.'

guerdon Reward or recompense.

For Nature also ... Matures the individual form i.e. natural selection.

Meet is it ... rust in ease i.e. it is right that we should be subject to constant change. See *Morte d'Arthur*, line 240: 'The old order changeth, yielding place to new,/And God fulfils Himself in many ways'.

A bridal dawn of thunder-peals i.e. change is not often brought about in politics without first enduring some sort of domestic upheaval.

warders of the growing hour i.e. the powerful rulers of the future.

Of Discord race the rising wind i.e. the disagreements of revolutionary change.

the brazen bridge of war i.e. no-man's land. See the *Iliad*, Book 8, line 553.

dogs of Faction i.e. bigoted followers of a dissident party or political creed.

Madeline (ME 27)

Another of Tennyson's female studies, published in 1830. The name 'Madeline' is associated with Keats's *The Eve of St Agnes*.

Madeline is changeable, unpredictable. She is a total mystery, yet she knows the lore of love. The poet is caught in her 'golden-netted smile' (another of those fanciful hyphenated epithets), but his advances result in a black disapproving frown.

silken sheeny woof The glossy threads or weft woven on to a warp in the process of weaving.

Margaret (ME 128)

Tennyson wrote this poem while at Cambridge, and it was published in 1832; it is a companion poem to 'Adeline'.

Margaret is melancholy, sweet and frail, completely detached from the strife and toil of life. The songs of Richard the lion-heart, the wild thoughts of Chastelard before the axe descended, mean nothing to her: she is impervious, her fairy shield protecting her from real sorrow. The poet begs her to listen to him as the lovely evening falls.

The lion-heart, Plantagenet The Plantagenet king, Richard I (Coeur de Lion), who was held captive at Durenstein (1192–3).

Chatelet Chastelard, the lover of Mary, Queen of Scots, who was beheaded in 1563. See *Chastelard*, a poetical tragedy by Algernon Swinburne, published in 1865.

leavy i.e. leafy.

Mariana (ME 23 OUP 54)

The poem is suggested by 'Mariana in the moated grange' from *Measure for Measure*, and by Keats's *Isabella*. It was first published in 1830. There is about the poem a sense of decay and pathos. Mariana weeps constantly because her lover will not come. She is weary she wishes she were dead as she waits for him in the lonely moated grange. By day she gazes across the gloomy fields, and by night still she waits. The sights and sounds from inside and outside of the house are her sole company, but she imagines voices and noises from the past.

Throughout this poem the reader is aware of her grief and loneliness, the hopelessness of her situation, knowing that her man will not return. All the while the grange decays around her; so too her life, until a solitary death seems inevitable.

trance i.e. entrance.

Upon the middle of the night This resembles closely Keats's line in *The Eve of St Agnes:* 'Upon the honey'd middle of the night.'

marish-mosses Tennyson describes this as the 'little marsh-moss lumps that float on the surface of the water.'

cell A reference to Milton's *Lycidas*, in which the cave of Aeolus appears.

thick-moted sunbeam i.e. the particles of dust visible in a shaft of sunlight as it streams through a window.

Was sloping toward his western bower In 1830 Tennyson originally wrote 'Downsloped was westering in his bower', which resembled too closely a similar passage from *Lycidas*.

Mariana in the South (ME 63)

First published in 1832, this poem originated during a journey with Arthur Hallam in the South of France; its location was between Narbonne and Perpignan. Tennyson the word-painter is splendid here, in his descriptions of the burning, dry, deserted, lifeless surroundings in which Mariana lives out her loneliness and despair. 'Alone', 'forgotten', 'forlorn' are repeated to fine effect throughout the poem.

And on the liquid mirror i.e. calm water. See Shelley's *Alastor*.

At eve a dry cicala sung The sound is more of a whistling rasp familiar on Mediterranean shores.

Hesper Hesperus, the planet Venus: the evening star.

The May Queen (ME 104); New-Year's Eve (ME 106); Conclusion (ME 109)

The famous lines 'You must wake and call me early, call me early, mother dear . . ./For I'm to be Queen o' the May, mother, I'm to be/Queen o' the May . . .' lend themselves to the composition of accompanying music and, of course, parody. Our May Queen has black eyes, which excel all others that will be celebrating the New Year.

Although 'The May Queen' was originally published in 1832, 'Conclusion' was added in 1842, appearing in the first of the two 1842 volumes.

In 'The May Queen' the wild and wilful girl thinks of nothing but of being crowned Queen of the May; cares nothing for the love of Robin, whose heart she callously breaks.

In 'New-Year's Eve' she is dying but prays that she will live long enough to see the flowers of spring before she is taken. Now that she is dying she admits 'I have been wild and wayward, but you'll forgive me now', and asks her mother's forgiveness.

In 'Conclusion' she is not yet dead, but the parson praying for her has shown her the light of God. She yearns once more for the flowers of spring, but now, knowing the peace of the Lord, she is content within herself and does not fear to go.

Charles's Wain Constellation of seven bright stars in *Ursa Major*, known as 'the Plough' or 'the Dipper'. The name has associations with the star-name *Arcturus* (for Arthur), and the legendary association of Arthur and Charlemagne (Charles the Great). What was originally called the wain of Arcturus became at length the wain of Charlemagne (an association not well-founded).

fallow lea uncultivated grassland

swallow ... o'er the wave The annual migration of swallows early in summer.

oat-grass Wild oats.

sword-grass Sharp-edged grasses, or reeds.

mignonette Fragrant flowers.

To lie within the light of God ... and the weary are at rest See Job, 3,17: 'and there the weary be at rest'.

The Mermaid (ME 55); The Merman (ME 53)

These two are mere ornaments in the *1842 Poems*. They were originally published in 1830 and are said to have originated in Walter Scott's *Minstrelsy of the Scottish Border*, which included John Leyden's *The Mermaid*: see Christopher Ricks's Notes in *Alfred Tennyson: Poems of 1842* (Macdonald & Evans). Hallam Tennyson quotes his father as having said, 'I never thought of Mermen and Mermaidens with tails.'

The Mermaid of the poem asks one question: 'Who would be/A mermaid fair ...', to which the Merman poses another: 'Who would be/A merman bold ...'

The main body of each of these two poems answers these rhetorical questions with imagery designed to titillate the senses and imagination, not to stimulate profundity of thought. They are merely trinkets for delight.

The Miller's Daughter (ME 71)

The setting of this idyll is quite obviously the southern end of the Lincolnshire wolds – probably in the area of Spilsby, through which Tennyson's famous brook the Steeping descends to Wainfleet All Saints, on its way to Croft Marsh and Wainfleet Sand where it flows into the sea. The poet's description of a mill is surely based on experience.

This uncomplicated poem, originally published in 1832, was thoroughly revised for the present edition. It is said to have been based on the idyll 'The Queen of the Meadow', by Mary Russell Mitford, which was reprinted in *Our Village* (1828) – a minor classic depicting village life at Three Miles Cross in Berkshire.

Spedding reviewed the poem in the *Edinburgh*, 1843, remarking that it is much enriched by the introduction of the mother of the lover.

Morte d'Arthur (F 128; ME 145)

Was Arthur a King? – There is strong evidence to show that he was not. He may, however, have descended from a well-born Roman family by the name of Artorius (spelt in a variety of ways). The Roman occupation of Britain was phased out and ended approximately in AD 446, whereupon foreign barbarians invaded the country, causing havoc and untold destruction. The *Historia Brittonum*, written about two hundred years after the events, relates that Arthur, who was born some time in the second half of the fifth century, was being employed as a *dux bellorum*, or Army Commander, in charge of a group of mercenaries. This mobile army, which protected Celtic tribes all over Britain from the Saxon invaders was, in fact, made up of cavalry survivors of the late Roman *eques cataphractarius* (who were protected with shirts of mail with the addition of arm- and leg-pieces). Chronicler Geoffrey of Monmouth (c.1100–54) asserts that in the course of his military duties Arthur visited Winchester, York and Lincoln, among other places. He is said to have fought in twelve battles, and at Mons Badonis he was largely responsible for the slaughter of 960 men.

It was Arthur and his cavalry who were instrumental in discouraging Saxon invasions for forty-five years. He was nicknamed 'Ursus' (the bear), because of his size, courage and strength. His coat-of-arms was originally silver with three lions turning their heads to their backs. He changed this to green with a silver cross, in memory of the crystal cross given him by the Blessed Virgin in the chapel at Beckery. But at last Arthur fell mortally wounded in battle at Camlann (various spellings). Dissension and jealousy had broken out among his own knights, and one of them, Medrant (also spelt Mordred), though himself dying had smitten him through the helmet, splitting his skull. The date of Arthur's death is said to have been 21 May 542, which indicates that he must have been well on in his fifties or even older, when his reflexes would have slowed considerably.

Morgain is said to have tended Arthur's wounds on the Isle of Avalon. According to a MS in the Cottonian Library, Arthur was 'piloted by Barinthus, skilled in the navigation of the seas and in the knowledge of all the stars of heaven, hither we brought Arthur sore wounded at the Battle of Camlin. With him as captain of our barque hither we came with our Prince; and Morgain received us with due honours, laid the king upon her couch covered with embroidered gold. With her own hand she uncovered the wound and examined it long. At length she declared that health might return if his stay with her be prolonged; and if he were willing to submit to her healing art'. Needless to say king Arthur died. But the legend is that he will return after a long sleep.

Arthur, it is claimed, was buried in the shadow of Wattle church, where Lancelot afterwards brought Guinevere. Hollinshed records that Glastonbury Tor, or the Happy Island of the Blest, is where Arthur was treated for his wounds. *Historia Regum Brittaniae*, the work of Geoffrey of

Monmouth, did much to perpetuate the legends and myths of Arthur, assisted in the fifteenth century by the romantic myths of Malory's *Morte d'Arthur*.

Arthur's remains were said to have been exhumed in the reign of Henry II on the Isle of Avalon. The king ordered that his grave be excavated. Seven feet down the diggers found a tomb upon which was fastened a cross of lead, 'grossly wrought', and on it was inscribed letters that included the name 'Arturius'. Nine feet lower was a sepulchre of oak made hollow, 'wherein the bones of that famous Arthur were bestowed'. Such methods of burial were the custom in the sixth century. Nearby were found those of Guinevere, whose body and gold-plaited hair were said to be in perfect condition. When the hair was touched it crumbled to dust. The relics were buried in the nearby church, remaining there for eighty-five years. The full inscription on the leaden cross was: *Hic jacet sepultus inclytus Rex Arthurus in Insula Avallonia* (Here lies interred in the Isle of Avalon the renowned King Arthur). The cross was deposited in the Abbey and was seen by Leland in the reign of Henry VIII, but was lost during the Dissolution.

Alfred Tennyson's comment on his 'Morte D'Arthur': 'How much of history we have in the story of Arthur is doubtful. Let not my readers press too hardly on details whether for history or for allegory.' It was not his intention that *Morte D'Arthur* should represent life and character in Britain in Saxon times. What we see in the *Idylls* is the chivalry of Norman and Angevin kings. The poet grafted nineteenth-century ideals on to the imagined ideals of the twelfth and thirteenth centuries. There is a glorious richness of illustration in the beautiful diction, music and rhythm. Details are painted with the absolute truth of touch. There is a grandeur of thought wrapped deceptively in the simplicity, vigour and expanse of his words.

Beginning with *The Lady of Shalott*, a lyrical romance, *The Idylls of the King* took fifty years to shape, re-shape and mould into the form that finally satisfied the poet. It is not certain in fact that Tennyson's eleven Arthurian books were burned, but at least *Morte d'Arthur*, *Sir Lancelot and Queen Quinevere* and *Galahad* survived to become incorporated, though transformed to 'epylls' (a combination of epics and idylls, containing the essentials of both forms) in the *Idylls*. Failure to publish others till 1859 was due entirely to John Sterling's review of the 1842 volumes in the *Quarterly*. Here is the chronology of the complete *Idylls of the King*:

1832 *Lady of Shalott* (which led to *Elaine*)

1842 *Galahad, Sir Lancelot and Queen Guinevere* and *Morte D'Arthur* (11 supposedly discarded) The latter became *The Passing of Arthur*)

1857 *Enid and Nimue: or The True and the False* (never published)

1859 New volume of *The Idylls of the King*, containing *Enid, Vivien, Elaine*, and *Guinevere*. *Enid* was then divided into *The Marriage of Geraint* and *Geraint and Enid* (the first volume contained the third, fourth, sixth, seventh and eleventh Idylls).

1862 New edition dedicated to the late Prince Consort with four more Idylls: *The Coming of Arthur, The Holy Grail, Pelleas and Attarre* and *The Passing of Arthur* (i.e. The first, sixth, ninth and twelfth Idylls).

1872 *Gareth and Lynette* and *The Last Tournament* (i.e. the second and tenth Idylls).

1885 *Balin and Balam*, an introduction to *Merlin and Vivien* (i.e. the fifth Idyll).

Therefore the final order of the Idylls was 3, 4, 6, 7, 11, 1, 8, 9, 12, 2, 10 and 5.

It is no mere coincidence, perhaps, that the poem 'Morte D'Arthur' published in 1842, was written when the poet himself was seeking, like Bunyan's Pilgrim, a view of the

gates of the Celestial City near the end of his spiritual pilgrimage (as described in *In Memoriam*, dedicated to his beloved friend Arthur Henry Hallam who had died in 1833.)
King Arthur stood for the ideals of royal wisdom, chivalric
virtue and knightly prowess; when Sir Bedivere has borne
the mortally wounded king to the awaiting barge to place
him in the care of his attendants, he cries in despair:

'Ah! my Lord Arthur, whither shall I go?
Where shall I hide my forehead and my eyes?
For now I see the true old times are dead,
When every morning brought a noble chance,
And every chance brought out a noble knight.
Such times have been not since the light that led
The holy Elders with the gift of myrrh.' (Lines 227–33)

The last two lines are a reference to the gospel of Matthew,
2,10–11. King Arthur replies with one of the most memorable passages from the Idylls:

'The older order changeth, yielding place to new,
 And God fulfils Himself in many ways,
 Lest one good custom should corrupt the world' (Lines 240–42)

He advises Bedivere to pray for his soul,

'. . . More things are wrought by prayer
 Than this world dreams of. Wherefore, let thy voice
 Rise like a fountain for me night and day . . .
 . . . the whole round earth is every way
 Bound by gold chains about the feet of God.
 But now farewell.' (Lines 247–56)

He tells Bedivere that when he prays for him and the old
order, he should remember that though men may imagine
they have free will, they are ultimately answerable to the
Divine Will of God; that is, 'bound by gold chains about the
feet of God'.

However, King Arthur consoles Sir Bedivere with his final

words, which seem to suggest that though his flesh is dying the spirit never dies. He is merely going to a place where his grievous wounds will heal.

'. . . I am going a long way
With these thou seëst – if indeed I go –
(For all my mind is clouded with a doubt)
To the island-valley of Avilion;
Where falls not hail, or rain, or any snow,
Nor ever wind blows loudly; but it lies
Deep-meadow'd, happy, fair with orchard-lawns
And bowery hollows crown'd with summer sea,
Where I will heal me of my grievous wound.' (Lines 256–64)

We are led to believe that the spirit of Arthur, the goodness, chivalry and Christian faith will be resurrected in men. It is possible that here Tennyson intends a deliberate analogy with the life and death of Jesus Christ, whose spirit is resurrected. King Arthur is the ideal man, without corruption, but is nevertheless the victim of the deceit and ambitions of some of his knights of the Round Table and of the unfaithfulness of his wife Guinevere in her affair with Sir Lancelot, his most trusted and valiant knight. In the same way Christ was pure and incorruptible, but was the victim of a corrupt society.

Tennyson's source for 'Morte D'Arthur' was of course principally Sir Thomas Malory's work of the same title printed by William Caxton in 1485. Another source was *The Mabinogion*, by Lady Charlotte Guest from 'the red book of Hergest', to be found in the library of Jesus College, Oxford. From it the poet fashioned 'Geraint and Enid'.

It will be noted that 'Morte d'Arthur' is in blank verse measured in iambic pentameters. The clever alliteration of the lines reflects exactly the sense, mood and music of the words. One remarkable passage exemplifies the poet's wizardry with sound-ornaments, when Sir Bedivere is carrying

Arthur to the waiting barque; we can almost hear his clanking footsteps on the jagged rocks, and the clash of armour:

Dry clash'd his harness in the icy caves
And barren chasms, and all to left and right
The bare black cliff clang'd round him, as he based
His feet on juts of slippery crag that rang
Sharp-smitten with the dint of armed heels –
And on a sudden, lo! the level lake,
And the long glories of the winter moon. (Lines 186–92)

The harsher vowels and consonants of the first five lines change in the latter two to the softer, gentler tones conveyed by *o*s and *l*s. Another example of his remarkable gift for word-painting is in the passage describing the sound and fury of wind and sea:

So saying, from the ruin'd shrine he stept
And in the moon athwart the place of tombs,
Where lay the mighty bones of ancient men,
Old knights, and over them the sea-wind sang
Shrill, chill, with flakes of foam. (Lines 45–9)

Lyonnesse A mythical land lying between south-west Cornwall and the Isles of Scilly.

Merlin Magician, prophet and mentor, who foretold that Arthur would become a great king and would return after death.

Excalibur The word means cut steel. The sword had magical qualities representing the invincibility of moral force. With it Arthur finds strength to form the Fellowship of the Round Table. In 'Morte D'Arthur', the king instructs Sir Bedivere three times to throw Excalibur into the lake. Eventually, reluctantly, he does so; it is caught by a hand emerging from the lake. See also Spenser's *Faerie Queene*, 'Prince Arthur': 'Thereby his mortal blade full comely hung/In ivory sheath . . .'

samite Rich mediaeval dress fabric of silk, occasionally interwoven with gold.

helm i.e. helmet.

jacinth A reddish-orange gem.

waterflags Water-irises.

fëalty Feudal tenant.

lief Glad, willing.

goad Something that torments, incites or stimulates.

stole A type of long, narrow shawl, worn over the neck, shoulders and arms.

casque A helmet.

greaves Armour for the shins.

cuisses Armour for the thighs.

Move Eastward, Happy Earth, and Leave (ME 273)

In *Poems of Lord Tennyson*, compiled by Sir Charles Tennyson (1954), this poem is entitled Wedding Eve, which is perhaps more appropriate than the above title. It was composed at some time between 1836 and 1838, most probably just after the wedding of brother Charles (Tennyson Turner) to Louisa Sellwood, Emily's sister. The marriage took place in May 1836. Alfred was best man, while Emily was brides-maid. It was during this auspicious meeting that Alfred and Emily recognized their love for each other.

silver sister-world i.e. the moon; note the reference to 'sister'.

Ode to Memory (ME 35)

This ode, addressed to an anonymous person, was influenced by Wordsworth's *Immortality Ode*, and was composed in 1830. In the fourth stanza the poet recalls his home at Somersby in Lincolnshire. Note that the archaic 'mine' – in the third from last line – is in this instance far more satisfying ono-matopoeically than 'my'.

Compare these lines with Wordsworth's in section 11 of *Ode, Intimations of Immortality from Recollections of Early Childhood*:

I love the Brooks which down their channels fret,
Even more than when I tripped lightly as they;
The innocent brightness of a new-born Day
                    Is lovely yet;
The Clouds that gather round the setting sun
Do take a sober colouring from an eye
That hath kept watch o'er man's mortality;
Another race hath been, and other palms are won.
Thanks to the human heart by which we live,
Thanks to its tenderness, its joys, and fears,
To me the meanest flower that blows can give
Thoughts that do often lie too deep for tears.

Both poets are reflecting nostalgically on the countryside of their birth – Tennyson is twenty-one, Wordsworth, the more mature, thirty-two. It will prove an edifying exercise to compare the two: Tennyson's pictorial description as against Wordsworth's philosophic view of the countryside and what it means to him.

Whilome The archaic form of 'once' or 'formerly'.
dew-impearled winds of dawn The whirling, dew-laden mists of dawn.
sere Sometimes spelt *sear*: withered, dried-up.
Pike Lakeland peak.
sand-built ridge Sand-dunes.
lowly cottage The Tennysons' Mablethorpe cottage on the coast of Lincolnshire.
Stretch'd wide and wild the waste enormous marsh The Fens.
descried Descriptive of the Pyrenees, which Tennyson and Arthur Hallam toured in 1830.
myriad-minded A mind teeming with many creative facets.

Oenone (ME 80; OUP 66)

Oenone ranks among the best of Tennyson's early classical and romantic poems. Published in 1832, it was revised for this edition. The earlier version was probably written in 1830–32, when Tennyson was touring the Pyrenees with Arthur Hallam. Oenone is an oread, or mountain nymph, who lives with Paris – a youthful handsome shepherd's boy who is in reality the son of King Priam of Troy – beside Mount Ida in that province. But Paris later deserts Oenone for Helen. The betrayed mountain nymph pines, broken-hearted. In 'The Death of Oenone', which Tennyson published in the last year of his life, he adapted the version of her death by Quintus Calaber.

The Irish poet Aubrey de Vere (1814–1902) believed that Tennyson's 'Oenone' was thoroughly Greek in spirit, 'though far richer in detail than the Greek art, a severe thing, as this commonly is'. The poet told Spedding in 1835 that 'of my old poems, most of which I have so corrected (particularly "Oenone") as to make them much less imperfect', he did not wish to expose himself again to criticism.

When comparing the original and later versions of the poem, Stopford Brooke, a brilliant preacher and author (1832–1916), comments: 'In the original cast, the scenery of the poem was not really interwoven with Oenone's mind. It did not fit her or feel with her as subtly and intimately as he wished.' In the later version, Brooke finds that 'at last we can no more divide Oenone from the Nature in which she is placed than we can separate the soul from the body of a friend. She is involved in the Nature which surrounds her, and the Nature in which she lives has mixed itself with her thought and her passion. Her constant cry, even in the first draft, proves this: 'O mother Ida, harken ere I die!'

Lines 142 to 148 are significant as representing Tennyson's personal philosophy.

vale in Ida Mount Ida in the Kingdom of Troas.

Gargarus The highest mountain in the range.

Troas The kingdom or region incorporating Troy.

Ilion Another name for Troy.

Paris Or Alexander, the son of Priam, King of Troy.

the golden bee/Is lily-cradled The bee sometimes becomes ensnared in the lily petals when they close during darkness.

as yonder walls/Rose slowly to a music Legend that the walls of Troy rose to the sound of Apollo's harp-music. (See also Note on *Amphion* (p.23) who was said to have raised the walls of Thebes with a lyre given him by Hermes.)·

Simois A Trojan river.

Hesperian gold Nymphs (known as 'the Hesperides'), were appointed to guard the golden fruit that Ge gave to Hera on the day of her marriage to Zeus. The garden was protected by a fearsome dragon.

Oread Mountain nymph.

Peleus Father of Achilles.

Herè Another spelling of Hera, the wife of Zeus. Her emblem was the peacock.

Pallas Athene, Greek goddess of Wisdom.

Aphrodite Venus, Greek goddess of Beauty and Love.

amaracus Marjoram.

asphodel Elysian flower.

guerdon 'Addition of reward' (Tennyson).

Idalian Aphrodite beautiful 'Idalium and Paphos in Cyprus are sacred to Aphrodite' (Tennyson).

her the Abominable Eris, the goddess of strife and discord.

Peleian banquet-hall The banquet hall of Peleus.

Cassandra King Priam's daughter. The gift of prophecy was bestowed on her by Apollo, whereupon she predicted the fall of Troy. However her prophecy was ignored because she rejected Apollo's advances.

'Of Old Sat Freedom on the Heights' (ME 137)

One of Tennyson's political poems, written in 1833. 'Of Old

Sat Freedom' takes a conservative stand on freedom. Though the poet wishes to see it spread through all classes of society, he eschews the 'falsehoods of extremes', Right or Left. Where freedom is concerned, Tennyson appears to come down staunchly on the side of the Establishment, setting great store by the lessons of history.

Stopford Brooke comments on his middle-of-the-road conception of freedom which avoids extremes: 'It is,' he said, 'that of the sturdy good sense of England, led to this conclusion by careful reasoning on the past, and by an intellectual analysis of the course of its history.'

Then stept she down ... with the human race Once again we see Freedom as a goddess taking on human form as 'to men reveal'd/The fullness of her face'. But it has taken them a thousand years to recognize her.

her isle-altar i.e. England.

the triple forks The spear carried by Britannia, the trident.

To —— With the Following Poem (ME 90)

This poem prefaces 'The Palace of Art' and was published in 1832. The poet's anonymous friend was R. C. Trench, one of the group or society of 'Apostles' to which both men belonged at Cambridge.

The 'Apostles' was a derisory term given to The Cambridge Conversazione Society by students outside its circle. Sir Charles Tennyson writes that it was represented by the new middle class which had arisen during the Napoleonic troubles in Victorian times, and which was to be responsible for shaping and governing England in the nineteenth century.

The argument in this poem evolved from a discussion between the 'Apostles' on Beauty, Knowledge, Good and Love – that the first three were worthless without Love, which was so often excluded from their company. The complete man

was created to possess Love as well as achieve perfection, or
Beauty, Knowledge and Good.

Howling in outer darkness Matthew 8,12: 'But the children
  of the kingdom shall be cast out into outer darkness: there shall
  be weeping and gnashing of teeth.'
common clay ta'en from the common earth Genesis, 2,7:
  'And the Lord God formed man of the dust of the ground, and
  breathed into his nostrils the breath of life; and man became a
  living soul.'

The Palace of Art (ME 91)

The poem is a dilation of the philosophy sketched in the
previous, accompanying poem. Van Dyke, in his *Studies in
Tennyson* (1966), says: 'The poem is an aesthetic protest
against aestheticism.' It reveals a broadening of the poet's
mind and allegorizes Tennyson's progression from the Cambridge cloisters and the elitism of the 'Apostles' to a view of the
universality of art. Art, in whatever form it appears, cannot
for long feed upon itself, but must inevitably decay if it fails
to associate itself with common humanity, and become part
of it.

  In 'The Palace of Art', first published in 1832, Tennyson
found his main analogy in Ecclesiastes, 2,1–17. It was based
on what R. C. Trench had said to him at Cambridge:
'Tennyson, we cannot live in Art.' This is precisely what the
poem attempts to prove through symbolism. Wordsworth
and Coleridge had come to a very similar conclusion in
1798, with the publication of the *Lyrical Ballads*: they intended to use the living language of the people, to return to
Nature for their inspiration. By degrees this was what
Tennyson was doing, trying to evolve from his academic
training by moving towards lyrical ballads.

  The poem shows the result of a selfish love of beauty – a
love of art for art's sake. The soul plans to live 'careless of

mankind'. The senses are satisfied but the heart is starved. It is a love of beauty similar to that of the Duke of Ferrara in Browning's 'My Last Duchess', unrelated to any obligation to one's fellows, unconnected with any moral influence on life. There is nothing wrong in the beautiful palace – the wrong is in the use to which it was put; when the palace is shared it can again become satisfying to the soul.

I built my soul Luke, 12,18: 'I will pull down my barns and build greater; and there will I bestow all my fruits and my goods.'

A huge crag-platform ... light Notice the number of pictures in this poem that are made to fit into a stanza.

or winding stair The natural word order is to place these words after 'shelf'.

Saturn whirls The planet Saturn revolves on its axis in ten-and-a-half hours.

luminous ring The 'halo' round the planet. Although Saturn revolves at such a rate there is no *appearance* of motion. Notice how Tennyson's observation of this astronomical phenomenon is as sure as his observation of the natural world.

sardonyx Onyx in which white layers alternate with sard.

Houris Maidens of the Mohammedan Paradise.

mythic Uther's deeply-wounded son i.e. King Arthur, wounded by Modred at Avalon.

Avalon The Paradise of the Arthurian heroes.

The wood-nymph ... the Ausonian king Numa Pompilius, second king of Rome, renowned as a law-giver, fell in love with the wood-nymph Egeria, who gave him the benefit of her wisdom for his laws. 'Ausonia' was the ancient name for Italy.

engrail'd Jagged.

Indian Cama Hindu god of Love, son of Brahma.

Europa A lovely Phoenician princess with whom Zeus fell in love. He took the form of a wild bull and came up to Europa as she was gathering flowers. Impressed by the animal's seeming tameness, Europa ventured to climb on its back, whereupon Zeus dashed into the sea with her and carried her off to Crete.

Ganymede A beautiful youth of Ohrygia. As he was tending his flocks on Mount Ida, he was carried up into heaven by an eagle at the command of Zeus, and became cup-bearer to the gods in place of Hebe.

Ionian father of the rest i.e. Homer.

Verulam Francis Bacon (1561–1626) was the first Baron Verulam.

Memnon A mythical King of Ethiopia, killed by Achilles in the Trojan war.

anadems Crowns.

Like Herod, when the shout was in his ears '. . . Herod, arrayed in royal apparel, sat upon his throne, and made an oration unto them. And the people gave a shout, saying, It is the voice of a god . . .' (Acts, 12,21–2).

Circumstance 'Some old writer calls the Heavens 'the Circumstance' . . . Here . . . a play on words.' (Tennyson).

The Poet (ME 43)

First published in 1830, the poem was revised for the 1842 edition. Tennyson delineates the qualities of a true poet, a hate of hate, a scorn of scorn and the love of love. To him the marvel of the everlasting will should be apparent.

The seeds of imagination take root and grow where they fall disseminating 'The winged shafts of truth' to fill the life of youth with hope. In this way, the poet multiplies truth, beauty and freedom, ideals advocated earlier by Keats. The sheer beauty of the last five stanzas should be studied closely.

Lines of iambic pentameters alternate with lines of varying syllables, with the rhyming pattern *abab*. However, as will be found elsewhere in Tennyson's work, there is cockney rhyming, for example: *tongue* and *sung*; *bore* and *flower*; *sunrise* and *eyes*; *thunder* and *wonder*; *sword* and *word* (eye-rhyming); and assonance like *whirl'd* and *world*. This is a habit, bad or otherwise, picked up from Keats, by whom Tennyson was influenced strongly at this stage.

Calpe Gibraltar, which the ancients regarded as world's end.
Caucasus The high mountain range between the Caspian and
 Black Seas.
lit Alighted.
arrow-seeds of the field flower The dandelion.

The Poet's Mind (ME 45)

The poem was first published in 1830. Tennyson was undoubtedly influenced by Keats's 'Lamia'. Do not, the poet
advises, attempt to interpret literally, or scoff at, the workings
of a poet's mind. His inspiration springs from holy ground. For
the poet, 'dark-brow'd sophistry' is anathema: his mind is
'bright as light, and clear as wind'. Cynicism and false creeds
are, inevitably, death to the imagination. Tennyson attempts
to describe the magic of the poet's mind: though its inspired
message is clear, the sophist would never understand, for his
ears are dull. He is warned away because he knows not the
purity of love and is foul with sin: 'It would fall to the ground if
you came in.'

The Poet's Song (ME 274)

Published in 1842, this poem was written when Edmund
Lushington married Tennyson's sister, Cecilia, which the poet
celebrated in the epithalamium of *In Memoriam*. There is now
definite evidence that Tennyson was taking a more optimistic
view of life – here he finds joy in everything.

the gates of the sun i.e. the East.
waves of shadow . . . wheat Notice Tennyson's close
 observation of a field of wheat in a breeze, rendered in an exact
 and imaginative metaphor.
The swallow . . . spray Notice the alliteration in this and the
 following line.
the down i.e. of his prey.

Recollections of The Arabian Nights (ME 30)

This poem was published in 1830 and appeared in Volume I of *Poems of 1842*. It incorporates two stories from *The Arabian Nights*: 'The History of Aboulhassen' and 'Noureddin and the Fair Persian'. One of Tennyson's first poems, it is purely descriptive; its value lies in its music, colourful imagery and sense of romance.

The poem is a day-dream of oriental splendours, revelling in detailed pictorial description, which, as in Mariana, owes much to Keats. Each stanza describes a new scene, first of all down the reaches of the river Tigris and its canals as the poet's shallop is carried onward, then, when he has left the boat, through the palace gardens, until finally he comes into the presence of the great Caliph himself.

Tigris A river in Turkey flowing south-east to join the Euphrates.
fretted gold Gold in ornamental patterns in delicate tracery.
shallop A light open boat.
citron A fruit resembling, but slightly larger than, a lemon.
broider'd Embroidered.
platans Plane-trees.
sward Smooth expanse of grass.
damask-work Embroidery woven with a figured design.
Imbower'd Confined in a leafy enclosure.
rivage Bank.
rillets Rivulets.
fluted vase Vase with semi-cylindrical groove cut vertically in it.
disks Discs.
tiars Tiaras: ancient Persian turban worn erect by king.
bulbul Eastern song-thrush, or a Persian nightingale.
grots Grottoes.
myrrh Gum resin used in perfumery and incense.
tamarisks Shrubs
Caliphat Muslim ruler.
twisted silvers Candelabra.
argent-lidded silver-lidded

rose-hued zone A girdle.
diaper'd Empanelled with ornamental designs of diamond
  reticulation i.e. with a network of small squares intersected by
  lines – in this instance with 'inwrought flowers, a cloth of gold'.

Sir Galahad (1842) (ME 243)

Published in 1842, *Sir Galahad* was written before 1834.
Tennyson said that it was intended for something of a male
counterpart to *St Agnes' Eve*.

  These are twelve-line stanzas with alternate rhyming.
Remarkable onomatopoeic effects are achieved as in lines 7/8:
'The splinter'd spear-shafts crack and fly/The horse and rider
reel'. The first and alternate lines are octosyllabic; the others
hexameters. Scansion and rhyming are identical to the
companion piece, *St Agnes' Eve*.

casques Helmets.
thrall Oppression or slavery.
censer Vessel for burning incense.
Three angels Intended to be the three Guineveres (see
  Tennyson's notes with *The Passing of Arthur* p.117).
mail Chain-mail armour.
holy Grail In the final *Idylls* the theme of this poem was
  expanded in *The Holy Grail* (1869), in which Percivale recounts to
  a fellow-monk, the story of the quest for the Holy Grail. The
  knight Bors has a vision of it – no more. Gawain fails completely
  to find it. Lancelot, while disentangling the noble elements from
  the one sin in his soul, also fails. The Grail, in mediaeval legend,
  symbolizes the vessel used by Christ at the Last Supper, in which
  Joseph of Arimathea received the Saviour's blood at the Cross.

Sir Launcelot and Queen Guinevere (ME 262)

Just as *Sir Galahad* was the companion piece to *St Agnes' Eve*, so
this poem is the counterpart to *The Lady of Shalott*. There are

nine-line stanzas rhyming *aaaabcccb* in octosyllabic metre. The only difference between this poem and *The Lady of Shalott* is in the lines 5 and 9 of each stanza; here they are not refrains. Hallam Tennyson informs us that it was written partly, if not wholly, in 1830, but we know from the manuscript that Tennyson was still working on it in 1833.

In this fragment Tennyson creates a fairy-land picture of idyllic countryside and woodland in the spring of the year, through which ride Sir Lancelot and Queen Guinevere. Indeed she is the personification of Spring in love with Sir Lancelot, who has given up everything to be with her. The fragment is what Stopford Brooke calls 'only a charming piece of glittering grace'. It underwent a metamorphosis in *The Idylls*.

throstle Thrush.
sparhawk Sparrow-hawk.
pastern Hoof.

The Sisters (ME 88)

Here is the story of two sisters, one fairer than the other. The less attractive sister is of violently jealous temperament, and when her more beautiful sister falls in love with an earl and disgraces their ancient blood, she seeks revenge by fire. This sister then sets out to seduce the handsome earl, first by inviting him to a feast and then by making love to him. They kiss and caress, and although she loathes him, she is curiously attracted by his beauty. That night, she stabs him to death, wraps his body in a sheet and lays him at his mother's feet.

This was published in 1832 and is said to be influenced by *The Cruel Sister* in Scott's *Minstrelsy of the Scottish Border*. The editor was reminded also of Browning's *Porphyria's Lover* in which a man greets his beloved from the storm and presumably to preserve her beauty and to keep her solely for himself, he strangles her with her hair, lying all night with her in his arms. Both lovers are insane.

The Skipping Rope (ME 272)

This simple twelve-line verse was written about 1836, first published in 1842, and reprinted from 1843 to 1850. Tennyson wrote it at the end of John Walker's *Rhyming Dictionary* (1800). It includes an index and under 'ope', are all Tennyson's rhymes: Antelope, skipping-rope, mope, hope. Alternate lines: by, eye, fly, sigh, die and thereby.

Song (F 110; ME 39)

This is in essence a song of the death of the year in late autumn, a delightful piece written early in the poet's career. Here we notice the influence of the Romantics. A spirit haunts the year's dying hours in the yellowing bowers. The poet grieves, his nostrils filled with the moist rich smell of the rotting leaves as he observes the year's last rose.

The essential melancholy of Tennyson's nature finds admirable expression in this song which rhymes, in the first stanza, *aabcdbba*, followed by the refrain *efgf*; in the second the rhyme is *aabccbba*, followed by the same refrain.

Song – The Owl (ME 28)

This song is particularly redolent of Shakespeare's 'When icicles hang on the wall' (*Love's Labour's Lost*): 'Then nightly sings the staring owl .../Tu-whit tu-who.'

The origin of the lines 'Alone and warming his five wits/The white owl in the belfry sits', is to be found in *King Lear*, III,3,56: 'Bless thy five wits! Tom's a-cold'.

The rhyming pattern of this song is *ababbcc*, as in the second song.

the whirring sail The revolving sails of a windmill.
roundelay This song, in fact, is a roundelay; that is, a bird's song, or brief simple song with a refrain.

The Second Song (ME 29)

Note the play on words 'Two wits' and 'tuwhits', 'Not a whit of thy tuwhoo,/Thee to woo to thy tuwhit,/With a lengthen'd loud halloo,/Tuwhoo, tuwhit, tuwhit, tuwhoo-o-o'.

Both these songs were published in 1830 and included in the 1870 *Juvenilia*.

St Agnes' Eve (ME 242)

St Agnes is the patron saint of virgins and was possibly martyred in the Diocletian persecution. Her festival is commemorated on 21 January. This poem was first published as *St Agnes* in 1836, and again in *The Keepsake* in 1837; the title was changed in 1855 to *St Agnes' Eve*. It describes the religious rapture of a virgin nun, and of how she is accepted by the Heavenly Bridegroom.

The poet's source here was William Hone's *Every-day Book*, and he comments that it was a pendant to *Sir Galahad*.

argent round i.e. the moon.
So in mine earthly house I am 2 Corinthians, 5,1.
For me the Heavenly Bridegroom waits Revelation, 21,9.
The Sabbaths of Eternity Hebrews, 4,9–11.
A light upon the shining sea Revelation, 15,2.

St Simeon Stylites (ME 174)

A dramatic monologue, this poem is, in Spedding's words, 'The pride of asceticism in its basest form'.

It is one of the three theological poems of the 1842 volumes, the other two being *Two Voices* and the *Vision of Sin*.

St Simeon Stylites has its origin in Simeon, a religious fanatic who perched himself on a pillar – stylites being the Greek for a pillar – remaining there for some thirty years. The ultimate aim is to subjugate the physical to the spiritual; to purge the body of all sin. The poet's sources here were William Hone's *Every-day Book*, and Chapter 37 of Edward Gibbons's *Decline and Fall of the Roman Empire*. J. H. Buckley believes that the poem may also have been influenced by a Cambridge preacher, Charles Simeon, whom Tennyson held in the greatest contempt. The poem was written in about 1833. The martyrdom of St Simeon Stylites is described in the iambic pentameter of blank verse.

The meed of saints, the white robe and the palm Revelation, 7,9.
this home/Of sin my flesh 2 Corinthians, 5,6.
Cover all my sin Psalms, 32,1.
O mercy, mercy! wash away my sin Psalms, 51,1–2.
A sinful man, conceived and born in sin Psalms, 51,5.
They think that I am somewhat Galatians, 2,6.
Can I work miracles and not be saved 1 Corinthians, 13,2.
Pontius and Iscariot Matthew, 26,14.
Abaddon Revelation, 9,11. Abaddon is the Hebrew name for the Greek Apollyon, angel of the bottomless pit.
Asmodeus Tobit, 3,8. Asmodeus, in the Apocryphal book of Tobit is the evil spirit who loved Sara, daughter of Raguel. Asmodeus causes the successive deaths of seven of Sara's husbands, each on his bridal night.
Mortify/Your flesh Colossians, 3,5.
yield not me the praise Psalms, 115,1.
a man of God 2 Timothy, 3,17.

The Talking Oak (ME 181)

'To me,' wrote Aubrey de Vere, 'the most delightful of these [idylls] is *The Talking Oak*. It is more difficult to make the

Manor House poetical than the cottage; but here, as in *The Princess*, and elsewhere, that arduous problem is solved. In it the poet's gift of expressive, harmonious and richly coloured language reaches its peak.'

Tennyson claimed it was an experiment meant to test the extent to which it was in his power as a poet to humanize external nature.

The poem was written about 1837 or 1838, and it was said to be influenced by *As You Like It*. The quatrains rhyme in alternate lines.

chace Unenclosed parkland.

plagiarised Imitated the human heart and mind.

garrulously Overly chatty.

Peter's-pence Papal tax abolished with the Dissolution of the monasteries.

Bluff Harry Henry VIII.

spence 'Monk's buttery' – A. Tennyson.

cowls The hoods of the robes worn by monks.

tho' I circle in the grain/Five hundred rings of years Each ring added to the circumference of a tree indicates a year's growth.

gamesome Gamely.

woodbine Honeysuckle.

anthers Part of stamen containing pollen.

Thessalian Of Thessalia in ancient Greece. The territory south of Mount Olympus and the River Peneus overlooking the Aegaean Sea.

The Two Voices (ME 211; OUP 104)

These octosyllabic triplets were begun in 1833 after the death of Arthur Hallam. The poet was so depressed he contemplated suicide; in his own words: 'When I wrote "The Two Voices" I was so utterly miserable, a burden to myself and my family, that I said, "Is life worth anything?" and now that I am old, I fear that I shall only live a year or two, for I have work still to do.'

The argument of the poem comes to this: 'Is life worth living? Were it not better not to be?' And the answer is, 'Life is worth living if life (with love) is eternal', and while the poet cannot *prove* it, he feels that it is.

five cycles . . . the sixth The six stages of creation, as given in Genesis, 1.

deficiency i.e. absence.

grass The comparison of man's short life with the withering grass (in a desert country) is a frequent one in the Old Testament, e.g. Isaiah, 40,6: 'All flesh is grass'.

Rapt after Rapt in following.

thirty seasons i.e. one generation.

lonely lights i.e. mountain tops smitten by the morning sun.

main Sea.

clay i.e. flesh.

toiling out his own cocoon i.e. each man makes his own ideas.

of Truth from his own particular experience Absolute Truth is unattainable.

fold i.e. the cloud.

Ixion In Greek legend, a treacherous king who was punished for his boast of having won the favours of Hera. Zeus had sent a cloud to Ixion in the form of Hera and by him the cloud became the mother of the Centaurs.

a little lower/Than angels See Psalm, 8,5.

Like Stephen The first Christian martyr.

The elements were kindlier mix'd In medieval times a man's temperament was supposed to depend on how the 'elements' or 'humours' (choler, phlegm, melancholy, blood) were mixed, or 'tempered' in him. The line is a reminiscence of Shakespeare's *Julius Caesar*, V,5,73.

Tho' one should smite him on the cheek See Luke, 6,29.

The place he knew forgetteth him See Psalms, 103,16.

yew A symbol of death.

Omega The end. See Revelation, 1,8.

He may not do the thing he would See Galatians, 5,17.

That I first was in human mould? That my first life on earth was as a human being.

Lethe One of the rivers of the Hades in Greek mythology from which the souls of the dead were made to taste that they might forget all they had done when alive.

lapsed from nobler place Living again in the world at a lower level of creation.

Moreover The comparison of this and the following stanza with Wordsworth's *Ode, Intimations of Immortality from Recollections of Early Childhood*, stanzas 5 and 9, is most interesting.

Æolian harp A harp so sensitive that when the wind blew through its strings it produced beautiful sounds. Æolus was the god of the winds in Homeric legend.

To (ME 26)

According to Tennyson, this poem was addressed at the outset to his friend J. W. Blakesley, a fellow student at Cambridge and later Dean of Lincoln. However, the character described became more a figment of the poet's imagination. It was written in 1830 and was later included in his *Juvenilia* (1870).

The poem's theme is the disentanglement of truth from falsehood, or 'Fair-fronted Truth' from sophistry. The poet looks on truth as a weak, fragile creature which must be fed by the intellect till it becomes 'an athlete bold'.

Sophist A captious or fallacious reasoner and quibbler. It derives from an ancient Greek teacher of philosophy and rhetoric (the Greek *sophistes*).

martyr-flames Burning at the stake.

trenchant swords Sharp or keen-bladed swords.

A gentler death shall Falsehood die Falsehood shall be defeated by cunning.

Like that strange . . . tract of Penuel This refers to Genesis,
32,22–31. Tennyson chose to alter the spelling of the original
Jabbock to Yabbock, the name of a river. Jacob had crossed the
river and wrestled with a man who dislocated his thigh. His
adversary renamed him Israel. The place where he stood was
named Penuel. Tennyson altered the *J* of Jabbock to Y to
conform to Hebrew pronunciation.

To J.M.K. (ME 57)

This sonnet to John Mitchell Kemble was first published in
1830, and was the only one to be included in the later *Juvenilia*.
Kemble was one of the Apostles at Trinity Cambridge, a great
friend of Arthur Hallam, Spedding, Tennyson and others of
that group. Because of his histrionic, volatile nature, he was
familiarly known as 'Black Jack'. Originally destined for the
Church, he forsook it for studies in Anglo-Saxon history and
literature, in which he was considered to be one of the
country's greatest authorities. He was a nephew of Mrs
Siddons and brother of Fanny Kemble, which is undoubtedly
where he inherited his theatrical temperament, his pug-
naciousness and grandiloquence. His humour was irre-
pressible, but sometimes he sank into a studied silence, and
when asked why, he replied invariably: 'The world is one great
thought, and I am thinking it.' Of Tennyson he had boundless
admiration: 'In Alfred's mind,' he once said, 'the materials of
the greatest works are heaped in an abundance which is almost
confusion'. Kemble narrowly escaped death when with others
from the Apostles, he went to help the revolutionaries in
Spain.

The rhyme-scheme of the sonnet is *abbacaacdededd*.

Luther Martin Luther, a German religious reformer
  (1483–1546).
soldier-priest So named because of Kemble's active support for
  the Spaniards.

sabbath-drawler ... old saws These were the antithesis of his
  nature.
worm-canker'd homily Old dreary sermon.
embattail To set in battle or array.
iron-worded proof Indisputable proof.
Arrows of lightnings Zechariah, 9,14.

To J.S. (ME 133)

Tennyson once said of James Spedding, to whom this poem is
addressed, that at Cambridge 'Spedding was the Pope among
us young men.' The poem was written in 1832, after the death
of James's younger brother, Edward, who was a great friend of
the poet.

  Tennyson distrusts tyranny on the one hand and unre-
strained individual liberty on the other – 'the falsehood of
extremes'. He believes in a liberty which consists in obedience
to a common law – 'sober-suited Freedom' (steady, ordered
progression, not revolutionary excesses), broadening down
'from precedent to precedent'.

  Notice the rhyme-scheme of the stanzas of each poem, and
the alternate rhyming of the quatrains, each line being
octosyllabic. Notice also the use Tennyson makes of personification.

The wind, that beats the mountain, blows The Lake
  District.
More softly round the open wold The Lincolnshire wold.
your holy woe The death of Edward Spedding, James's younger
  brother, and the poet's friend.
Once thro' mine own doors Death did pass His own father's
  death in 1831.
to weep or not to weep Reminiscent of Hamlet's suicide
  speech.
God's ordinance God's decree.

Ulysses (F 91; ME 194; OUP 88)

The impression given by these lines is that the poet had already conquered his grief over Arthur Hallam's death; but not so. It was written a few weeks after he received the tragic news in October 1833. The poem is in fact a soliloquy in the Homeric manner, a gallant attempt to boost his own spirits, to restore his courage and brave the struggle of life.

Ulysses is the epitome of heroic leaders in all ages from ancient Greece to modern times. Tennyson was chiefly inspired by Dante's *Inferno* (26), but the theme was of course based on Homer's *Odyssey*.

Tennyson picks up the story where Homer's *Odyssey* ends. As prophesied by Teiresias, Ulysses yearns to travel again, and the poem opens as he addresses the sailors who originally accompanied him on the Odyssey. These men had in fact drowned in a shipwreck, but Hallam comments that his father had intended that Ulysses's new comrades in Ithaca were to accompany him, and that they were of 'the same heroic mould as his old comrades'. Although Ulysses is made to speak in the iambic pentameters of blank verse, being a warrior with a vision, his words are nonetheless very stirring.

an aged wife i.e. Penelope.

mete and dole The words have a sense of littleness and pettiness. Nothing open-handed is implied.

know not me i.e. cannot understand my restlessness for travel and adventure (because they are concerned merely with laying in store for the body).

lees Dregs.

Hyades Seven nymphs, daughters of Atlas and Pleione whom Zeus placed among the stars. Legend has it that they wept so bitterly at the death of their brother, that Zeus was moved to take them up to Heaven.

I am a part . . . met i.e. my experiences have helped to make me what I am.

Yet all . . . move i.e. travel breeds an impulse for more travel, not for settling down; however much one travels the 'untravelled world' remains like the horizon, which can never be reached but recedes as one moves towards it.

Life piled on life i.e. many lives.

three suns i.e. three years, the little span of life which, as an old man, he can now expect.

Telemachus The son of Ulysses and Penelope.

soft degrees i.e. gentle steps.

strove with Gods i.e. in the Trojan war.

the Happy Isles Believed to be beyond Gibraltar.

Achilles Greek hero, son of Peleus and the goddess Thetis. To make him immortal, Thetis took the infant Achilles to the waters of the Styx. Holding him by the ankles she dipped him in the river, but forgot to immerse his heels. At the siege of Troy, Achilles slew Hector but was subsequently killed himself by an arrow from the bow of Paris, which struck his heel.

The Vision of Sin (ME 265; OUP 124)

Tennyson himself informs us that this poem, believed to have been written after 1839, describes the soul of a youth who has given himself up to pleasure and Epicureanism. The poem comes into a group of four: *A Vision of Sin* itself, which discusses the moral effects of over-indulgence in pleasure; *The Palace of Art*, which is a warning against excessive love of beauty in art and intellectual pride; *St Simeon Stylites*, which satirizes the excesses of theological asceticism; and *The Two Voices* which advises against the morbid introspection that can lead to suicide. All these experiences had been an intimate part of the poet's own life and Tennyson felt it his duty to warn others to beware of them.

This is an allegory about a young rider arriving at a castle mounted on the winged horse of his aspiration and imagination which have become weighed down by the desires of the flesh. Sin accompanies him into the castle and so indulges this weakness with sensual pleasure that when he eventually leaves, he has become sated with it, and cynicism has transformed his personality.

At this point, section 4 changes to quatrains with alternate-rhyming lines. The youth sees himself when old, and recognizes this unhappy vision of what he might be: the incurable Epicurean; shameless and malicious; an alien to love and goodness; a misanthropist and a hater of himself – a soul sour with cynicism.

Section 5 of the poem changes key again. Suddenly this revolting image of himself as a degenerate old man dawns upon him because he is not totally lost. From this we infer that the youth was partially restored to grace in the eyes of God. What Tennyson is saying, in effect, is that like all human beings we tend, unless we discipline ourselves, to take pleasures or indulgences to excess; this, he believed, should be avoided at all costs. Observe, for example, his political poem, 'Of Old Sat Freedom on the Heights'. This applies equally in theology, in art and in emotional and intellectual over-reaction.

gourds Types of melon.
Furies The avenging deities in Greek mythology.
Graces In classical mythology the goddesses of beauty and charm.
ostler Stableman at an inn.
rouse Carouse; drinking bout.
shards Potsherd.
dross Rubbish, impurities.
God's likeness See Genesis, 1,26.
Far too naked to be shamed See Genesis, 2,25.

Walking to the Mail (ME 171)

This was something entirely new in English poetry: a dialogue carried on in intelligent but uncomplicated language between

John and James. It was written about 1833 and seems to be emulating the easy, conversational English of the Romantic revival used predominantly by Wordsworth, but with a humourous flavour to it. It is an essay in poetic drama in miniature, containing character studies and descriptions of the countryside. The poet is illustrating how external influences, whether perpetrated innocently, or otherwise, can change one's life or personality for better or for worse.

broken Bankrupt.
younker Youngster.
this bill that past i.e. the Reform Bill (1832).
That these two parties i.e. the Whigs and Tories.
Niobe According to Greek legend the wife of Amphion and mother of fourteen children. She taunted Latona who had but two children and as a result, all her children were destroyed.

Will Waterproof's Lyrical Monologue
(ME 247; OUP 121)

Subtitled 'Made at the Cock', the character in this poem portrays 'the plump head-waiter of The Cock, by Temple Bar, famous for chop and porter . . .' though it appears that the head-waiter was rather offended when told of the poem – *Will Waterproof*.

  Written in about 1837, there is about this poem the haze of alcoholic humour nurtured in the fellowship of old comrades. One can almost smell the smoke-laden air, the wine and the steaming food; and hear the ceaseless chatter and clinking of glasses. There is something almost Falstaffian in this carouse, the prolixity of intoxicated humour.

Lusitanian Portuguese.
But for some true . . . work together Romans, 8,28.
raffs rabble, disreputable persons.

As on this whirligig . . . the seasons *Twelfth Night*, V,1,376.

Temple-bar Where the Strand and Fleet Street meet.

stiffer More potent.

peptics Digestive glands.

Waterloo i.e. the battle fought in 1815 near Brussels.

Canning George Canning entered Parliament 1793, became
  Prime Minister in 1827 (1770–1827).

Ganymede Ganymede, a beautiful youth carried by an eagle
  from Mount Ida to tend Zeus as cup-bearer in place of Hebe.

Sipt wine . . . in golden barley As a cock drinks raising his head
  to heaven as though in prayer.

something-pottle-bodied Pot-bellied.

knuckled at the taw Playing marbles.

thorpe Village, hamlet.

smoky Paul's St Paul's Cathedral.

thrumming Tapping with his glass idly on the table.

sherris 16th-century spelling (origins) of Spanish sherry

ana Anecdotes, literary gossip.

maudlin-moral A mawkish, sentimental stage of drunkenness.

allots Distribute by lots.

unctuous lease/Of life Fawning (as with Uriah Heep in *David
  Copperfield*).

'You Ask Me Why, Tho' Ill at Ease' (ME 136)

This poem and '*Of Old Sat Freedom on the Heights*' come into a
special section of their own, with *Love Thou, Thy Land*; these
were all pre-Laureate pieces, inspired solely by a love of the
country. They could well have done for laureate poems. In
fact they first appeared in 1833, inspired by the Reform Bill
of 1832.

Revision Questions on Part One

1 Compare and contrast any two of Tennyson's early
poems, paying particular attention to the poetic techniques
used.

appreciation in some detail of *The Day-Dream*.

account of Tennyson's use of myth in any two

4 By what means does Tennyson create a particular atmosphere in either *The Lotos-Eaters* or *The Lady of Shalott*?

5 Consider Tennyson's use of nature in any three or four poems.

6 In what ways is Tennyson not merely lyrical but intellectual? You should refer to a range of poems in your answer.

7 Write on Tennyson's attitude towards art *or* human suffering in any two poems.

8 Write an appreciation of Tennyson's use of Arthurian or classical legend in any poem or poems.

Part 2

The Princess

In the mid 1840s, after the collapse of the wood-carving enterprise in which Tennyson had invested most of his money, he had a total breakdown and was forced for a period to enter a hydropathic establishment. But at this time he was offered a £200 annual pension by Sir Robert Peel, which may have contributed to his recovery.

Tennyson began work on *The Princess* which was to be an allegory of his times: it describes a university founded by a noble fanatical girl that is to be kept free of male contamination. Treatment was to be light, poetical and imaginative. Scenes of power and pathos alternate with the exquisite lyrics, of which we have a sample in this selection. There were flashes of burlesque in the poem, and many readers were uncertain whether they should take the work seriously or not.

Princess Ida is contracted from birth to marry the Prince of a Northern allied kingdom. The marriage at first fails to materialize because Princess Ida, an independent minded young lady, is fanatical in her resolve to create a university solely for ladies where men are not allowed. At this time, in England, there was much talk of freedom, independence and self-determination for women in society and in education, and this allegory, though with a fairy-tale quality, aimed to support that ideal. But Tennyson's wholehearted sincerity about the scheme is not entirely convincing.

The Prince infiltrates the university in disguise, is discovered, and in a rescue bid by the Prince's armed forces, is wounded, as are many others. The university is turned into a hospital, and while the Princess tends his wounds, she falls in love with him, and marries him, thus proving that love is stronger than the powers of the intellect.

from **The Princess**

'Tears, Idle Tears' (F 114; OUP 132)

This is considered to be one of Tennyson's finest lyrics, and was certainly one of his favourites.

The poet has cleverly experimented with blank verse in the five-line stanzas, and possibly he had A. H. Hallam in mind when writing it. By nature the poet was a melancholy fellow at times, and the poignancy and pathos of these lines are accentuated by the devices of euphonious vowels and consonants, e.g. the repetition of 'tears' in the first line; the words, 'depth', 'divine' and 'despair' in the second; and 'eyes' and 'rise' in the third.

By the judicious use of alliteration and assonance within the lines, he has dispensed with the need for end-of-line rhyming.

In 'To *dying* ears, when unto *dying eyes*', he repeats the drum-beat dirge of the *d* and *y*. Note the sibilant and soft consonants in line two of the last stanza. 'Ears' and 'eyes' moreover, have a linking assonance, and both are vehicles of the senses, melodious, sad and haunting.

Tears, Idle Tears was written at Tintern Abbey. The poet confessed that the poem did not express real woe, as some people might have supposed, 'it was rather the yearning that young people occasionally experience for that which seems to have passed away from them for ever.' In him it was strongest when a youth.

'O swallow, swallow' (OUP 133)

This, the Prince's love song, was, according to Hallam Tennyson, originally composed in rhyme, and later changed to blank verse when first published in 1847

Note the euphonious use of consonants and vowels, notwithstanding the lack of rhyme: the s, w, l and th, and the warm vowels for the swallows flight south; and the harsher br, erc, the fickle and the trill of the South – 'And cheep and twitter twenty million loves.' The Prince compares her delayed love toward him with the tardiness of the ash tree to send forth its shoots in the Spring. She had best hurry to him because the summer is brief in the North, but brief too is 'the moon of beauty in the South'.

'Now Sleeps the Crimson Petal' (F 114; OUP 134)

Here is another of those delightful feather-weight songs from *The Princess*. It is a short piece, delicate, colourful and transparent as the princess sings to her lover, the prince.

You will find no profound thought here, only the haunting vision of love's reaction to, and total communion with, the beauty of Nature. It may be useful to study the poem's construction to understand how the poet achieves the overall effect:

1 The *sleeping* crimson and white petals.
2 The *stillness* of the cypress in the palace walk.
3 The *immobile* goldfish in the stone font.
4 The firefly *awakening, awakens* love.
5 The effect produced by the *ghostlike milkwhite peacock*.
6 The earth, *like Danaë*, ravished by the stars.
7 The *silent meteor like a plough* leaves its *trailing furrows of light* through the *black ether of the universe*.
8 The lily, *enfolding its sweetness* within itself, sinks into the *bosom of the lake* – the natural consummation.

The final stanza of four lines completes the cycle of images as the lily folds its loveliness within itself, as love absorbing beauty into itself becomes an entity.

porphyry A very hard ornamental Egyptian stone with a basic colour of red embellished with white and red feldspar.

Danaë It had been told that Danaë's son would kill his mother's father Acrisius, but Zeus showered her with gold and she became the mother of Perseus of the winged feet.

'Come down, O maid' (OUP 135)

Tennyson considered this Idyllic song to be among his most successful work for simple rhythm and vowel music. He wrote it in Switzerland chiefly at Lauterbrunnen and Grindelwald. It describes 'the waste Alpine heights and gorges, and the sweet, rich valleys below'.

The poet tells the maid to come down from her cold, lofty mountain wastelands, which reflect her frosty nature to the warmth and sunlight and plentitude in his valley where Love dwells.

Metaphors and epithets abound in this poem. For example, the vivid images in 'red with spirted purple of the vats/Or foxlike in the vine'. One can almost taste the grapes, see the red, and feel the stickiness of them. The metaphor is almost three-dimensional. And again, who else but Tennyson could have written 'and spill/Their thousand wreaths of dangling water-smoke,/That like a broken purpose waste in air'? Anyone who has travelled through mountain regions will appreciate those startlingly realistic images, and almost feel the drifting spray from the falls on his face.

'The Splendour Falls' (F 113; OUP 136)

This fairy-tale lyric was added to the 1850 edition of *The Princess*. Unlike most of the previous lyrics included in the work, this and 'Ask Me No More' are in rhyming stanzas.

Here we have the internal rhyming *'falls* and *walls*; *shakes* and *lakes*; *hear* and *clear* etc. There is also end-of-line rhyming *abcbdd*, the last two lines of each stanza being the refrain, though they do not repeat one another, word for word, e.g. 'Blow, bugle, blow' and 'answer echoes, dying, dying, dying'.

'Ask Me No More' (OUP 136)

This lyric and *The Splendour Falls* were published in the 1850 edition of *The Princess*. Unlike their predecessors each lyric rhymes. In 'Ask Me No More', the title is the refrain throughout, and the bewitching music tends to bemuse one's understanding of it. A similar refrain will be found in Thomas Carew's *Song*: 'Aske me no more' is the first line of each stanza.

The imagery has a fairy-tale quality about it – 'The cloud may stoop from heaven and take shape/With fold to fold, of mountain or of cape' – if separated from the main body of the poem, but if read in context, the meaning becomes a little clearer. The two hosts from the North and South kingdoms have fought; the women's university has been invaded and violated, and the clamour of horses hooves and chariots and armour can be heard. The wounded have been taken into the hospital, once the university, but the Prince has been locked in a deep chamber 'shut from sound'. He prepares to die from his wounds. He hopes in vain that Princess Ida will love him.

To ——, After Reading a Life and Letters (OUP 137)

This appeared first in the *Examiner* with the Shakespearean epitaph: 'Cursed be he that moves my bones.' It was in fact a hit at Lord Houghton for publishing in 1848 the private letters of the poet Keats. 'My father,' wrote Hallam Tennyson in his *Memoir*, 'was indignant that Keats's wild love-letters should have been published; but he said that he did not wish the public to think that the poem had been written with any particular reference to *Letters and Literary Remains of Keats*. He placed Keats "on a lofty pinnacle" among the poets.'

In these lines Tennyson admits that if Keats had lived he might have become an even greater poet. But his life was so short he had missed 'the irreverent doom/Of those that wear the Poet's crown'. Keats was now immortal, but even before he was cold in his grave, his *Relics* were being unearthed. Though neither statesman nor king, Keats' private life was now being pried into. His Shakespeare's curse on those who would not let him rest.

from In Memoriam

In Memoriam was written in memory of Tennyson's friend, Arthur Henry Hallam. The separate elegies of which it is composed were written at irregular intervals between then and its publication in 1850. Though nominally to the memory of a particular friend, the poem is an impersonal lyric, or rather series of lyrics. It is not the direct expression of a wild and piercing grief: it is in a tranquil, melancholy strain. From it we gather little of Hallam's personality, and in it we have no record of the times the two friends spent together. The only one we know better at the end of the poem is Tennyson himself.

The real subject of *In Memoriam* is not the death of Hallam: it is the death of *anyone*, the sorrow of those who remain, the mystery of a life which is thus ended, the relation of the individual to the universe, and the hope of immortality.

Tennyson shows clearly how desperate had been the struggle to preserve his faith, to free himself from the Slough of Despond and to view life more philosophically. But how to reconcile the premature death of a dear, gifted friend, of no more than twenty-two years, with the concept of a loving God? The only answer must be a blind, unquestioning faith, however irrational it may seem to the human mind.

In Tennyson's own explanation of the poem, he reminds the reader that it is *not* an actual biography; that it is founded on friendship, the engagement of Arthur Hallam to his own sister, on Hallam's sudden death at Vienna prior to their marriage and on his burial at Clevedon Church in Avon.

This poem more than any other was the reason for Tennyson's appointment as Poet Laureate. Tennyson's simple expressions of religious faith came not a moment too soon in the moral destiny of the nation, because after 1859 many of the basic Christian tenets were to be questioned seriously in the light of Charles Darwin's theories on the evolution of life in *The Origin of Species*. Tennyson, like Darwin himself, believed that the theory of evolution could be made compatible with Christianity, although many contended that it undermined the Old Testament.

In Memoriam should be read, and better understood, in conjunction with *Break, Break, Break* (p.26), *Ulysses* (p.87), and *Crossing the Bar* (p.123), examples of some of the finest of Tennyson's lyrics in which his inspiration is fired by a divine faith in the *living* God and a oneness with Nature. The poet's religious beliefs were influenced, here, by Arthur Henry Hallam's work *Theodocaea Novissima* (1831). There is, also, a clear analogy between *In Memoriam* and the *Sonnets* of Shakespeare, which were addressed to an unknown young man, though any hint of homosexuality on his part was strongly refuted.

Prologue (F 135; OUP 139)

This is a summation of Tennyson's metaphysical pilgrimage, or, as he preferred to call it, 'The Way of the Soul'.

The Prologue was the last section to be written in 1849. In it Tennyson addresses the 'Strong Son of God'. He reasons that though He is spiritual and unseen, we must still have faith in His existence. He has created Life and Death and deals equally fairly with both. Life is incomprehensible for why must man die? Nevertheless if it is God's will, so be it, for He is just. Although our wills are ours, yet are we bound by the divine will of God. Our nations and governments are ephemeral and transient, of little consequence when compared with His kingdom which endures. Our faith must be blind, but as knowledge is acquired, so faith increases. When we are foolish enough to deny him without fear, we mock him.

The poet seeks forgiveness for grieving over the loss of Arthur Hallam for so long, but he now believes that his friend lives in the divine God of Love. He seeks forgiveness, too, for his wild cries of grief and especially where he had deviated from the truth. He asks the God of wisdom to make him wise.

Thou madest Life in man and brute See John, 1,3.

thou art just And it would not be just to make him merely so that he could die.

systems i.e. sects, creeds and dogmas.

broken lights By refraction.

For knowledge is of things we see See Romans, 8,24.

what seem'd He is no judge. He therefore asks forgiveness for what he distinguished as his 'sin' and his 'worth' in his own eyes.

I trust he lives in thee Notice the 'I trust'. All through this prologue there is a sense of groping after an assurance that he would fain have but cannot grasp.

VII (F 14; OUP 140)

'Dark House' refers to Arthur Hallam's house at 67 Wimpole Street. He had remarked to his friends, during his stay there, that they would always find him at 'sixes and sevens'. But now gloom and despondency fills the poet's mind at the sight of the wet, dismal street, and the dark house where his friend will never stay again.

XI (F 15; OUP 141)

The calm and beauty of the autumn morning fill him only with calm despair.

XV (F 15; OUP 141)

Winter sets in. The winds roar, the red leaves scatter and the rooks are blown about the sky. So, too, is he in a 'wild unrest that lives in woe'.

Athwart a plane of molten glass See Job, 37,18.

XIX (OUP 142)

This section was composed at Tintern Abbey, beside the River Wye, and it refers to Arthur Hallam's death in Vienna and the voyage home by ship to Clevedon.

Danube Vienna, where Hallam died, is on the River Danube.
twice a day the Severn fills This, of course, refers to the twice-daily incoming tides when sea-water mingles with the river.

XXXIV (OUP 143)

There must be life after death, says the poet, or life is mean-

ingless and worthless. This beautiful world in which he lives
might have been created by a fanciful poet like himself without conscience or aim. What then was God to such as he?
Surely it is better to concentrate on the tangible world rather
than to try to understand the spiritual, to live life and die,
dropping into vacant darkness.

XXXV (OUP 143)

If only there could be a voice from the grave (the 'narrow
house'), someone trustworthy, denying that death is anything but dust and decay.

the narrow house i.e. the grave.
Æonian hills Everlasting hills.
forgetful shore Perhaps Lethe, or, as Tennyson put it, 'The
  land where all things are forgotten'.
Satyr-shape Satyr was a Greek deity in human form with
  horse's ears and tail. He was a lustful, greedy man.

L (F 16; OUP 144)

He pleads with his friend to be near him in spirit, now that
he is so despondent, when his faith fails him.

LIV (F 17; OUP 145)

He trusts that there is a divine purpose in life (as every
winter changes to spring), but in our ignorance it seems a
dream only.

pangs of nature Natural instincts.
sings of will Deliberate sins.
Defects of doubt Failure in belief, scepticism.
taints of blood Hereditary weaknesses.
night . . . light Symbolical of ignorance and knowledge.

LV (OUP 145)

Here is a loss of faith but a desire to believe in immortality, as in the last stanza of this section.

And gather dust and chaff An attempt to reason.
the larger hope The phrase was explained by the poet to his son, that 'the whole human race would through, perhaps, ages of suffering, be at length purified and saved'.

LVI (F 18; OUP 146)

We are led to believe that God is love, but nature seems 'red in tooth and claw', confounding His creed. Life seems futile, frail. What hope is there for a voice to speak to him from beyond the grave, to soothe and bless his spirit?

Who trusted God was love indeed See John, 1,4.

LXVII (OUP 147)

The moonlight shines on him as he lies awake and he suddenly visualizes it shining also on Hallam's name inscribed on a plaque in the chancel of the little church overlooking the Severn. Then all is dark, and the mystic vision fades with the moon. But when he awakes next morning he again imagines the name on the plaque as it 'glimmers to the dawn'. (See *The Princess*, 7,165–6: 'Now droops the milkwhite peacock like a ghost,/And like a ghost she glimmers on to me').

LXXXVI (OUP 148)

This was written at Barmouth, Merioneth, Wales, during the spring of 1839.

ambrosial Of ambrosia, the food of the gods.
brake Thicket, brush.
dewy-tassell'd Droplets on leaf and bough after a shower.
horned flood 'Between two promontories' (*Tennyson*). See also
  Milton's Paradise Lost, 11, 827.
From belt to belt ... orient star i.e. the west wind rolling to
  the Eastern seas till it meets the evening star.

XCI (F 19)

It is March, and the poet asks his dead friend to appear to
him as he remembers him – in the Spring of his life, full of
promise. And, in summer, come, he pleads, not to haunt him
in the night, but in the golden sunlight.

XCV (F 19; OUP 148)

Left alone one beautiful summer's dusk, a hunger seizes his
heart, and 'silent-speaking words' seem to test his worth; the
spirit of his dead friend touches him from the past. Suddenly
the living soul is flashed upon him – he is caught up and
lifted to 'empyrean heights of thought', and he senses the
'deep pulsations of the world', as though he were an ethereal
being. But as suddenly, his doubts return. Are these merely
words, the intellect reaching through memory? Then the sun
rises and the lights of life and death broaden into 'boundless
day'.

word by word, and line by line See Isaiah, 28,13.

C (F 21)

He returns to places he and his friend had once enjoyed
together; but still the pangs of grief beset him.

CI (F 22; OUP 151)

The glories of summer go unwatched, unloved, uncared for, and the memory of his friend fades. In sections C to CIII the Tennysons leave Somersby.

CVI (OUP 151)

It is New Year's Eve (possibly 1845–6), a time for rejoicing at the death of an old year and the birth of a new, replacing the false with the true. Be gone grief, he says, and the feud between the rich and poor. Dispense with dying causes and party strife. Ring in nobility, good manners and purer laws. Death to want, care, sin, the faithless coldness of the times; an end to pride in place and blood, and to the civic slander and spite. Replace all these with love of truth, right and common love of good. Cure foul diseases and lust for gold. Stop wars and bring peace. Welcome the valiant and free, the large-hearted and kindness. Replace evil with Christ.

Ring in the thousand years of peace Revelation, 20,2–4.
Ring in the Christ that is to be 'The broader Christianity of the future' (Tennyson).

CXV (F 23; OUP 153)

Early spring awakens his soul, to blossom like the flowers. Here his spirit blossoms with the life of the world.

burgeons every maze of quick Sets budding every tangled hawthorn bush.

CXVI (OUP 153)

Will he always feel in April the same nostalgia and longing for former times? No, the spirit is reawakening like nature all about him. When alone he will still recall Hallam's face and voice, yet he experiences less sorrow now, less yearning for lost friendship than for some strong future liaison.

crescent prime 'Growing spirit' (Tennyson).
re-orient out of dust Resurrected spirit.

CXIX (F 24)

As the city sleeps he smells the scents of the countryside. He regards the past without sadness and he feels the presence of his friend's spirit about him. He has revisited Wimpole Street. The physical loss of Hallam is not now so painful.

CXXIII (F 24; OUP 154)

In a constantly changing, evolving world, his dream remains constant, and he will never forget. The essence of man is spiritual – the only reality.

CXXIV (F 25; OUP 154)

Though faith sometimes fails him, the failure is transitory because now a fundamental belief in the God of Love fills him. But he remembers his moments of doubt and fear. No proof of his faith can be given.

CXXVI (F 26)

His faith is fully restored in the God of Love and through him he hears the tidings of his friend, and in the depth of night he senses that all is well.

CXXX (OUP 155)

The poet imagines he hears Hallam in the air and water,

sees him in the rising sun and feels a diffuse power from him, but loves him none the less. It is a vaster passion in a mystical communion with God and Nature. His spirit is far and near at one and the same time, and he senses that it will always be thus.

This is analogous with Shelley's *Adonais*, which was dedicated to the memory of Keats.

Thou standest in the rising sun Revelation, 19,17.

Come Not When I am Dead (F 112)

This poem was first published in *The Keepsake* in 1851. The disillusioned or disenchanted lover speaks to his former sweetheart telling her not to visit or weep needlessly over his grave, but 'there let the wind sweep and the plover cry'.

He has no recriminations for what happened; if it were her error or her crime, he knows not and no longer cares – 'being all unblest'. She should now wed whom she may. He personally is weary of life and seeks only rest. He is weary after the anger of love, but still feels an underlying tenderness towards her. She must pass by and forget him.

The two six-line stanzas rhyme *ababcc* and the last two lines of the second stanza rhyme with those of the first. All other lines vary considerably in length.

Considering that Tennyson has only been married one year, this is a remarkably morbid poem. There can be only one explanation that he was addressing Rosa Baring, his one-time sweetheart. Her relations deemed themselves a cut above the Tennysons of Somersby, and when the poet and Rosa had been caught embracing, they were forbidden to meet again. Harrington Hall where the Barings lived is said to be the 'Hall' in the poem *Maud*, and his expulsion left the poet very bitter, because he loved her deeply. Indeed this provides part of the theme for *Maud* (see p.112).

Ode on the Death of the Duke of Wellington
(F 119; OUP 156)

Here we have Tennyson's voice speaking from the heart of the nation, expressing completely its sentiments of determined patriotism. Tennyson, like his fellow-countrymen, did not want war. He abhorred it and the death and destruction that would inevitably follow in its wake.

Some critics like Stopford Brooke, however, believed that Tennyson over-reached the bounds of his poetic duties on occasion, as in Section VII of the *Ode on the Death of the Duke of Wellington*. He felt the poet was too patriotic, too exclusively English, and too controversial.

But with a few reservations, such as the over-playing of the Duke's virtues as against his weaknesses, this ode was seen to be a great work of art. There is a variation in flow of the metrical movement. Its rhythm matches the meaning of the verse. In Section VI, the swelling harmony reaches its climax when the spirit of Nelson, that 'Mighty Seaman', asks from his grave, 'Who is he that cometh, like an honour'd guest . . .'

Popular though the Ode was, it never received the widespread acclaim, however less deserved, of *The Charge of the Light Brigade*, which was inspired by a tragic blunder in the Crimean War of 1854.

pall A cloth spread over coffin, hearse or tomb.
statesman-warrior Wellington (1769–1852) fought in India, in the Peninsular War and was appointed ambassador to Paris in 1814. He then fought at Waterloo, after which he was appointed Prime Minister from 1828 to 1830. For ten years, until his death, he was Commander-in-Chief. He was buried in St Paul's.
cross of gold Cross on the dome of St Paul's.
myriads of Assaye The hordes of the Mahratta's army in India.

Round affrighted Lisbon drew The Peninsular War in 1810, when Wellington constructed the ramparts of Torres Vedras. In the following year his army defeated the French (they lost 25,000 men) and drove them back into France.

On that loud ... spoiler down Battle of Waterloo 18 June 1815.

Baltic and the Nile Nelson's naval victories of 1801 and 1798.

England's Alfred King Alfred.

shining table-lands Revelation, 2,23.

Ashes to ashes, dust to dust Genesis, 3,9.

To E.L. on his Travels in Greece (F 136)

In 1853 Tennyson was married with one boy, Hallam, and another, Lionel, soon to be born in the following year; travelling was now out of the question. What is more, the family moved into Farringford in the Isle of Wight that year.

Therefore when the poet reads an account of Edward Lear's travels in Greece, he is envious, having only two years previously travelled with Emily through Italy – a happy memory (see *The Daisy*).

Lear the artist, musician and writer of nonsense poetry, was one of the group of friends who was always welcome at Farringford, especially by the children. The bond of friend-ship between the two men was forged back in 1841.

At the time of his terminal illness in 1888 Lear was preparing for publication 130 landscape engravings of Tennyson's poems symbolizing or expressing indirectly their spirit and meaning.

However Lear died before the completion of his work and only 36 were issued on condition that Tennyson signed 100 copies, which he did most reluctantly.

There are, in this dedication to Lear, six stanzas rhyming *abba*, each stanza being made up of four lines.

E.L. Edward Lear (1812–88).

Illyrian woodlands Illyris, now Albania, in north-west Greece; a province beside the Adriatic.

Peneïan pass Through which the River Peneius flows in Thessaly. In Greek mythology Peneius was the son of Oceanus and Tethys, and father of Daphne and Cyrene.

Athos Regarded as a holy mountain situated on the promontory of Chalkidike in Greece. Site of a monastery.

Naiads Water mymphs.

The Charge of the Light Brigade (OUP 166)

Popular as was the *Ode to the Duke of Wellington*, it never received the widespread acclaim, however less deserved, of *The Charge of the Light Brigade* which was inspired by a tragic incident in the Crimean war of 1854.

The poem was published in *The Examiner* on 9 December 1854. On 6 August 1855 Tennyson had a request from Scutari to send specially-printed copies of the poem so that the troops could see them. This he gladly did, and indeed the poem was very popular at the front.

An interesting comparison may be made between this poem and Browning's *How They Brought the Good News from Ghent to Aix*, illustrating how both poets conveyed the effect of horses' galloping hooves in desperately urgent circumstances.

It had been suggested to the poet that he had Drayton's *Ballad of Agincourt* in mind when writing the poem, but Tennyson refuted this suggestion. Suggestions have also been made that he subconsciously remembered Chatterton's *Song to Aella*, which goes 'Down to the depth of Hell/Thousands of Dacyanns went'.

The Daisy (F 106)

This is not an over-impressive poem, except for the metre. It is little more than a versified travelogue – an artist's rapidly executed water-colours portraying details of places seen en route by the Tennysons on their Grand Tour of Italy in 1851. How much better it would have been done by either Browning, Shelley or Byron.

Tennyson was ill in bed at Edinburgh when he wrote this poem. He addresses his wife, Emily, recalling the tour of the previous year. He remembers that he plucked a daisy near the summit of Splugen. But now that Hallam their son was born they could travel no more.

Feeling ill and weary, alone and cold, he finds the daisy, crushed and hard, in a book Emily had lent him. Suddenly he fancies that the clouded Firth of Forth, the gloom of the city, the bitter east, the misty summer, the grey metropolis of the North are all forgotten. Instead they are both in the warm South again.

Each stanza has four lines rhyming *aaba*.

amaryllis Kinds of bulbous plants.

Columbus Born in the vicinity of Genoa (1446–1506).

oleanders Wild olives.

Genovese People of Genoa.

Cascinè At Pisa, Italy.

Lodi Town on the River Adda, Italy.

Monte Rosa The highest peak in the Apennine Alps, Italy.

Como Lake Como, in Northern Italy.

Virgilian rustic measure . . . Lari Maxume *Larius*: Book 2, line 159. The Como omnibus was called the *Lariano*.

To that fair port i.e. Varenna.

Agavè Probably referring to the plant which takes sixty to seventy years to mature and blossom.

Splugen In the Rhaetian Alps, between Lombardy and Grisons, Switzerland.

So dear a life your arms enfold A reference to the poet's elder son, Hallam, who was born in 1852.

clouded Forth i.e. the Firth of Forth.

And gray metropolis i.e. Edinburgh.

Maud (F 26; OUP 168)

Briefly the story of *Maud*, a romantic narrative or mono-drama, in which the first canto begins with four-line iambic stanzas, rhyming *abab*, is about the passionate love and madness of the narrator. His father was ruined financially by Maud's father, and then loses his life either by his own hand or by another's. Our hero believes it is suicide and he becomes a highly nervous, half-hysterical person, often gentle, often violent from weakness, living on the edge of the supernatural. He is morbidly excited by what he takes to be his father's suicide, by his lonely life and he broods on those commercial iniquities which ruined his father. A childhood love had existed between our hero and Maud, who returns with her brother from abroad to the Hall. Though Maud knows the cause of the suicide and has a strong filial affection, she renews her love with our hero.

The brother catches Maud and her lover together, and challenges him to a duel. The brother is killed, and Maud's love for our hero dies with him. To escape her wild cries and haunting image, her lover, near mad with grief, flees to Brittany, where he slowly recovers his sanity, and finally becomes embroiled in the Crimean war against Russia.

It was the last part of *Maud* which caused a furore of criticism when the poem was first published in 1855. Many readers were misled into believing that Tennyson was praising the war. Even the most astute critics, Stopford Brooke and Gladstone, failed to see that the character was largely a fictional one, and these were not sentiments which Tennyson himself would have entertained, though he did sometimes get carried away with patriotic fervour. Tennyson explained to Henry Van Dyke at Aldworth the process of character-building in the piece and the difficulties of portraying madness in a fictional character – especially in verse.

It was intended to show the unfolding of a 'lonely, morbid

soul, touched with inherited madness, under the influence of a pure and passionate love'. What seemed like faults in it were merely stages of development – 'each lyric is meant to express a new moment in the process'.

Tennyson does not agree with our hero when he implies that war will change him into a great-souled hero, or will lessen dishonesties and the miseries of war.

Our hero's actions are wild, excessive. When first he expresses his love, he lacks nobility: he strikes a false note and strains the tone of passion to the point of hysteria. Trifles preoccupy him, and he becomes 'fantastically merry'. And who should know better than Tennyson himself who was brought up in a family suffering from melancholia and morbid moods; whose father was driven to the verge of insanity by those very moods and drink. The poet had been heart-broken on at least two occasions when both Rosa Baring and Emily Sellwood had turned him down. He had seen madness at first-hand when he invested in the mechanised wood-carving enterprise at the Epping Lunatic Asylum where he met John Clare the poet.

All these biographical details were invaluable to him in his portrayal of madness, heartbreak, passion and rage.

The form in *Maud*, as a monodrama, is novel, and allows Tennyson great metrical freedom. Henry Van Dyke points out, in his book, that the conversational style of writing was seen to be unconventional; the attacks on industrial systems antagonized the middle classes; and the eulogy of war scandalized the radicals.

Stopford Brooke found that solving the problems of Maud's lover by sending him to fight in someone else's war in the Crimea, was the main flaw in the poem.

wann'd Paled.
worldling Worldly person.
spirit of Cain 1 John, 3,12.

my heart as a millstone Job, 41,24.

set my face as a flint Isaiah, 50,7.

we are ashes and dust Genesis, 3,19.

when only not all men lie Psalms, 116,11.

vitriol Poison, caustic speech.

alum A mineral

Mammon Matthew, 6,24.

yardwand Rigid yard measure.

neither savour or salt Matthew, 5,13.

spleen Ill-humour.

transient Ephemeral, impermanent, passing phase.

scream of . . . by the wave The pebbly beach of Freshwater
 Bay sounds like this when sucked down by the undertow.

Orion A bright constellation. Orion's belt consists of three
 bright stars close in line. Tennyson was a keen astronomer, and
 often watched the stars through a telescope from the roof of
 Farringford.

Czar England was then involved in the Crimean war against
 Russia.

epicurean A pleasure-seeker.

rapine Plundering.

eft Newt.

knout A Russian whip, often fatal for the victim.

wannish Pale.

coquettish Flirting insincerely (to ensnare him).

dandy-despot Well-dressed or over-dressed autocrat.

hustings Election proceedings for parliament.

Viziers High officials in Muslim countries.

dilettante Amateur lover of the Arts.

gewgaw A bauble or gaudy plaything.

splenetic Ill-tempered.

rancorous Spiteful.

huckster Hawker, peddlar.

opulence jewel-thick Showy wealth.

contumelious Insolent.

Gorgonised A stare that metaphorically turned him to stone.
 From Greek mythology: the snake-haired woman whose looks
 turned victims to stone. She was known as Medusa.

huge scapegoat of the race Leviticus, 16,10.

bower A leafy enclosure.

ramps Is rampant.

roystering i.e. roistering, or uproarious revelling.

hasp A window-fastener.

Oread Mountain nymph in Greek mythology.

thrall Servant or slave.

dry-tongued laurels' pattering talk Describes exactly the sound of laurel leaves flapping together as they are stirred by a summer's breeze. There were laurels in the grounds of Farringford.

Gates of Heaven Revelations, 21,21.

Dark cedar The poet wrote some of *Maud* beneath a cedar in the gardens of Swainston. Genesis, 2,8.

mattock-harden'd hand Here the poet was no doubt talking from experience, because he himself tended the garden at Farringford and developed callouses on his hands.

sad astrology Is modern astronomy; old astrology was thought to sympathize with and rule man's fate.

Not die but live a life of truest breath This is the central idea, the holy power of love.

woodbine Honeysuckle.

musk Smell as of the musk-rose.

jessamine Jasmine.

Wraith Ghost.

vassals Holders of land by feudal tenure.

whorl A scalloped circle as with petals of a flower.

Lamech Genesis, 4,23.

I never whispered a private affair Luke, 12,3.

Tithonus (F 93; OUP 90)

Written in the classical vein, *Tithonus* is in blank verse of Homeric iambic pentameters. The story is based on the Greek legend of a beautiful Trojan youth called *Tithonus*. Brother to Laomedon and beloved by Eos, *Thithonus* prayed to the goddess to grant him immortality. He unfortunately forgot to ask for perpetual youth and as he grew old, life became unbearable to him. He now prayed to Eos to remove him from the world; the goddess was unable to do this but she did transform him into a cicada (a transparent winged shrill chirping insect that haunts the Mediterranean shores).

Apollo God of prophecy, music, healing; son of Zeus and Leto.

The Eagle (F 111; OUP 156)

In this fragment the rhyming is *aaa, bbb*. In the first line we have the harsh consonants, c, r and k; in the second, the warmer and softer l and n, and the vowels a, o and u; returning in the third line to the consonants r, g, z, s and t, conveying the grandeur and sweep of the eagle's view of the world. In the fourth we envisage, from on high, how remote the country below must seem to it – the rippling waves, like sand at the ebb tide, merely 'wrinkled'. Everything seems to move slowly from a height, hence the word 'crawls'. Ultimately the eagle surprises us with a sudden swoop 'like a thunderbolt', in its deadly swift descent, from his mountain walls.

The poem was first published in *Poems* in 1851.

'Flower in the Crannied Wall' (OUP 191)

This fragmentary piece of six lines was composed at Waggoners Wells, near Haslemere, and published in 1869. It has the simplicity of some of Burns's lines – a moment of wonder as he pauses at the roadside to pluck a flower, root and all, from a cranny.

The Passing of Arthur (OUP 175)

Students should refer to the notes on page 60 regarding

Morte d'Arthur published in 1842. It formed a large portion of *The Passing of Arthur* (issued in 1869 as the concluding section of *The Idylls of the King*). Lines 1–169 and 441–69 were added to the original *Morte d'Arthur* to provide continuity with the preceding section (*Guinévere*) and to conclude the *Idylls* as a whole.

Tennyson said it was 'The temporary triumph of evil, the confusion of moral order, closing in the Great Battle of the West'. Before studying it, students may wish to read *The Epic* (p.36) which precedes *Morte d'Arthur*.

Hallam Tennyson writes in his *Memoir*: 'My father felt strongly that only under the inspiration of ideals, and with his "sword bathed in Heaven", can a man combat the cynical indifference, the intellectual selfishness, the sloth of will, the utilitarian materialism of a transition age. "Poetry is truer than fact," he would say. Guided by the voice within the Ideal Soul looks out into the Infinite for the highest Ideal and finds it nowhere realized so mightily as in the Word who "wrought with human hands the creed of creeds." But for Arthur, as for everyone who believes in the Word however interpreted, arises the question "How can I in my life, in my small measure, and in my limited sphere reflect this highest ideal?" From the answer to this question come the strength of life, its beauty, and above all its helpfulness to the world.'

In the Garden at Swainston (OUP 191)

During his lifetime Tennyson loved three men more dearly than any other. These were Arthur Henry Hallam, Harry Lushington and Sir John Simeon, who prevailed on the poet to write *Maud*. The poet outlived them all by many years.

The poet looked upon Sir John Simeon as a brother, and when the news came of his death at Friburg on 23 March 1870, it was a terrible blow, not only to the poet, but also to his family. On 31 March the poet attended the funeral at Swainston, and while the coffin lay in the house, he took one of his friend's pipes with him to smoke in the garden and there beneath the cedar, which had featured in *Maud*, he wrote *In the Garden at Swainston.*

To Edward Fitzgerald (F 115)

Although dated 1876, this poem, dedicated to Tennyson's old friend Fitzgerald, was written much earlier. Fitzgerald in 1876 lived at 'The Grange', Woodbridge in Suffolk. He is remembered best for his *Rubaiyát of Omar Khayyam* from the Persian which he published anonymously in 1859. He also made English versions of the 'Agamemnon' of Aeschylus and of the two 'Oedipus' tragedies of Sophocles.

The friendship between the two men went back to the 1830s, when 'Fitz' recalled hearing Tennyson quote some lines from the early version of *Morte d'Arthur* in 1835 while resting on his oars in the middle of Lake Windermere.

There had always been a deal of chaffing and light-hearted banter between them, not to mention teasing criticism of each other's work. Their friendship has been compared with Horace and Virgil, 'Fitz' being the lazy Epicurean, Virgil. 'Fitz' himself had great poetic gifts, but an unhappy marriage and an indolent attitude to life and his work. He was a fine critic, but recognized his limitations, his 'crochets' and prejudices.

Tennyson said of him: 'I have no truer friend; he is one of the kindliest men, and I have never known one of so fine and delicate a wit.' 'Fitz' died before this poem was published. On his epitaph was written: 'It is He that hath made us and not we ourselves'.

As if they knew ... meal and grass This is a reference to the fact that Fitzgerald was a vegetarian. Acts, 10,11.

Pythagoras Sixth-century Greek philosopher who believed in the transmigration of souls and the blood brotherhood of men and beasts. He abstained from all flesh foods.

thing enskied *Measure for Measure*, I,4,1.

grapes ... Eschol hugeness Numbers, 13,23.

and from two ... all the rest James Spedding and W. H. Brookfield, who died 1881 and 1874 respectively.

The Revenge (F 100)

This, a remarkably stirring ballad, evokes the spirit of the Elizabethan age. The chant of the ringing metre carries us with it, as spellbound, we plunge in the tiny *Revenge* into the midst of Spain's fifty-three men-of-war, the high castles of their galleons dwarfing us below.

The *Revenge*, with Sir Francis Drake as commander, had played a successful part in the defeat of the Armada in 1588. He was succeeded by Sir Richard who, in 1591, was sent with six other fighting ships and six commercial vessels to the Azores to intercept Spanish vessels bearing gold and silver to Spain. They had received rumours of Spaniards coming from South America. However, while the English were watering, replenishing vessels and tending the sick sailors, Spain sent fighting ships under the command of Don Alfonzo Bazan to protect their interests. Many of the English crews were sick and ashore, so Lord Thomas, rather than be caught in harbour by the Spaniards, decided that discretion was the better part of valour and set sail. But Sir Richard refused to be hurried, and remained in harbour until nearly all his sick men had been brought aboard. By now, however, he was separated from the rest of the English vessels, and though the *Revenge* herself had time to escape the Spaniards, Sir Richard decided to fight it out, so low was his opinion of their seamanship. Tennyson's historical source for the poem came from a then recently published reprint of Edward Arber's material on the subject.

Flores Most north-westerly of the Azores Islands.

Azores Portuguese islands in mid-Atlantic, 900 miles (1440 km) west of Lisbon.

Sir Richard Grenville (1541–91) Vice-admiral and second-in-command aboard the *Revenge*.

Lord Thomas Howard Admiral-in-command; nephew of Lord Howard of Effingham, the Lord High Admiral in charge of the English fleet opposing the Spanish Armada in 1588.

Seville A province and its capital port in Spain, on the River Guadalquivir.

San Philip The flagship of the Spanish fleet which attacked the *Revenge*; commanded by Don Alfonso Bazan.

musqueteers Soldiers armed with muskets.

Queen Elizabeth I.

Rizpah (F 137; OUP 194)

Tennyson related that *Rizpah* was founded on an incident which he had read once in some penny magazine called *Old Brighton*, lent him by a friend and neighbour, Mrs Brotherton.

The poem itself is a ballad, a dramatic monologue which many consider to rank with *Revenge* and *The Ode on the Death of the Duke of Wellington* as one of his finest pieces written late in life.

From poetic drama for the stage, Tennyson had returned, late in life, to the monodrama form which his reading public preferred. Van Dyke reminds us that the ballad is based on the Hebrew story of a mother watching beside the dead bodies of her sons whom the Gibeonites had hanged on a hill. For six months, night and day, she defended them from wild beasts and birds of prey. *Rizpah* therefore is a dramatic paraphrase from the Bible. It is a noble tragedy, full of desperate pathos, expressing how deeply she loved her sons.

In the poem the mother is shut in gaol and fastened to her

bed, where she remained year after year till she was believed
to be insane. On her release, she secretly collected the bones
from the gibbet, kissed them and buried them in the sancti-
fied ground of the churchyard. This moving drama proved
to the poet's faithful readers that his powers had not gone
into decline.

Rizpah 2 Samuel, 21,8–10.
As the tree falls so must it lie Ecclesiastes, 11,3.
Flesh of my flesh ... bone of my bone Genesis, 2,23.
My Willy 'ill ... 'ill sound 1 Thessalonians, 4,16.
Full of compassion and mercy Psalms, 86,15.

To Virgil (OUP 192)

This ode was written in June 1882 at the request of the
Virgilian Academy of Mantua on the nineteenth centenary
of the poet's death. He lived from 70 to 19 BC, and his chief
works were the *Aeneid*; the *Georgics*, a didactic poem; and
the *Eclogues* and *Bucolics*, imitations of the pastorals of
Theocritus.

In the *Aeneid*, a poem in Latin hexameter, Virgil recounts
the adventures of Aeneas from the fall of Troy, and how the
Trojans settled in Italy.

Ilion Troy.
Dido Elissa, daughter of a Tyrian king, married her uncle, who
was murdered for his wealth. She escaped with it from Tyre to
Carthage, where she burned herself to avoid having to marry a
neighbouring king. Virgil makes her a contemporary of Aeneas
with whom she falls in love, when he is shipwrecked near
Carthage. When the gods order Aeneas to forsake her, she
burns herself on a funeral pyre.
Tityrus Or Tityre, or Tittyry, taken from the first words of
Virgil's first Eclogue '*Tityre, tu patulae recubans sub tegmine fagi.*'

Pollio Gaius Asinus, a Roman consul to whom Virgil dedicated his *Eclogue iv*, in which the birth of Christ is predicted.
Northern Island Britain.
Mantovano Mantuan.

'Frater Ave Atque Vale' (OUP 194)

In 1880 Hallam Tennyson and his father were in northern Italy. 'From Verona,' wrote Hallam in his *Memoir*, 'we returned home by the Lago di Garda [Lake Garda] and Milan. Over Sirmio, the peninsular of Catullus, we roamed all day. My father liked this, I think, the best of anything we had seen on our tour: its olives, its old ruins, and its greensward stretching down to the blue lake with the mountains beyond. Here he made his *Frater Ave atque Vale*.'

Catullus's *Ave atque Vale*, written for his dead brother, reflected in Tennyson's lines the memory of his own brother Charles's death in the previous year. And in *Sirmio* is an expression of joy on homecoming, 'Peninsularum, Sirmio, insularumque Ocelle.' (*Catullus*, 32,1)

Early Spring (F 117)

Two versions of this poem exist. The first was published in 1833; the second in 1883 lacking the five stanzas ii, iv, vi, viii and ix. But even those which were republished were rearranged and revised. The two versions afford us a rare opportunity of comparing Tennyson's poetic powers early and late in life. They confirm the verdict already reached of an evenness in his work from beginning to last.

No doubt he had good reasons of his own for omitting these stanzas, but one feels he could well have left out some of the more laboured stanzas included in the 1883 version.

Makes all things new Isaiah, 65,17.
A Jacob's ladder falls Genesis, 28,12.

Vastness (OUP 200)

First published in 1885 for *Macmillan's Magazine*, this poem returns to the poet's much discussed theme: 'What matters anything in this world without full faith in the immortality of the Soul and of Love?' Concern about the Soul's immortality had preoccupied him all his life. This poem preceded his serious illness of 1888–9 when he at last became convinced of a spiritual life after 'Crossing the Bar'.

Innocence ... mother's milk Exodus, 34,26.
He that has nail'd ... the Cross Galatians, 5,24.
The dead are not dead, but alive Matthew, 22,32. Mark, 12,27.

Crossing the Bar (F 143; OUP 203)

Crossing the Bar was written in Tennyson's eighty-first year. Though normally he composed slowly, the lines this time had come to him in a flash of inspiration during a ferry-crossing of the Solent from Lymington to Yarmouth. Without mentioning them to anyone he had jotted them down on an old envelope, and in his study at Farringford, he had later copied them out afresh with minor corrections.

He had been very near to death in the past few months, and his recovery had seemed miraculous. His nurse, Durham, had suggested he wrote a hymn of thanksgiving, but instead he composed himself to see his 'Pilot face to face'. Time for him, he believed, was running out.

In the poem, Tennyson gives thanks to God for curing him miraculously of his illness; indeed his gratitude is too deeply felt to be expressed adequately in words. The flood tide which originally bore his soul to the shores of Life is now ebbing, returning it to the boundless depths of the Eternal from whence it came.

In the third stanza he speaks to his dear ones, beseeching them not to be sad at the last; to have courage enough to overcome the sadness of personal loss, just as he had also done after the deaths of Hallam, Lushington, Simeon and his own son, Lionel.

For though in death he will be far away from them, beyond their mortal dimensions of Time and Place, at least they should seek consolation in the fact that he, in spirit, hoped to see his God face to face.

It has already been said that, although the poet had attained great reverence for the past, his reverence for the present was even greater. This is shown conspicuously in the poem *Crossing the Bar*, in which his inspiration is fired by a divine faith in the *living* God. His son Hallam Tennyson told him that it was the crown of his life's work. His father explained that the Pilot was 'That Divine and Unseen Who is always guiding us'. He asked that the poem may always be placed at the end of all editions of his poems.

The poem consists of four quatrains, alternate lines rhyming *abab*. The metre is iambic, but the number of feet per line varies extensively from stanza to stanza.

bar Sandbank or shoal across a harbour-mouth or estuary. Here symbolizing the divide between life and death.
evening bell The ship's bell.
bourne Meaning broadly-speaking dimensions or mortal limits.
flood Full tide.
Pilot God.
I hope to see my Pilot face to face… 1 John, 3,2.
  1 Corinthians, 13,12.

Revision questions on Part Two

1 What are the main concerns of *The Princess* and in what form does Tennyson express them?

2 Consider any two or three of Tennyson's songs, bringing out their main poetic qualities.

3 In what ways is *In Memoriam* both personal and universal? You should refer closely to two or three different sections of the poem.

4 Write a study of Tennyson's use of verse form in *In Memoriam*, saying whether you find the usage monotonous or not.

5 Write a detailed appreciation of the narrative and poetic techniques which Tennyson employs in *Maud*.

6 Write a detailed appreciation of any single poem in this section.

7 Write a considered appraisal of Tennyson's treatment of *either* age *or* public events in this section.

8 Consider Tennyson's use of formal versification in any poem in this section.

General questions

1 What qualities make Tennyson a fine lyrical poet? You should refer to at least four or five poems in your answer.

2 Write an appreciation of Tennyson's narrative art in two of the longer poems.

3 In what ways does Tennyson's poetry reflect the main concerns of the Victorian age?

4 'A fine eye, and a finer ear'. How accurately does this sum up Tennyson's art?

5 In what ways do you consider that Tennyson is the poet of pessimism?

6 Write an essay in defence of the charge that Tennyson's poetry is concerned almost exclusively with the past.

7 Write an essay on Tennyson's use of any particular poetic form, indicating what qualities he brings to it.

8 What dramatic qualities do you find in Tennyson's verse? You should refer to two or three poems in your answer.

9 In what ways is Tennyson a philosophical poet?

10 'A facile versifier'. In what ways is Tennyson much more than this?

11 Which of Tennyson's poems in this selection indicate that he took the position of Poet Laureate seriously?

12 'His main concerns are loneliness and melancholy'. How far is this true of Tennyson's verse?

13 In what ways may Tennyson's poetry be described as 'romantic'?

14 'It is the sound that matters, not the sense'. Would you agree or disagree with this assessment of Tennyson's verse?

15 What qualities in Tennyson's poetry make him stimulating for today's readers? You should refer to a range of poems in your answer.